Advanced LBO Masterclass by VCII

The Dealmaker Playbook

ALBOM

The Definitive Guide

from Fundamentals to AI

Value Creation Innovation Institute

MeriTIP

MeriTIP Publishing

Table of Contents

Introduction

Welcome to the *Advanced LBO Masterclass: The Dealmaker Playbook.* This comprehensive guide, authored by VCII, is designed to equip private equity professionals, aspiring financiers, and strategic thinkers with the tools, frameworks, and insights necessary to excel in the complex world of leveraged buyouts (LBOs). From foundational principles to cutting-edge innovations like AI-driven analytics, this resource bridges the gap between theory and practice.

Leveraged buyouts represent the pinnacle of financial engineering and strategic execution. They combine high-stakes decision-making, intricate deal structuring, and relentless value creation. This masterclass is tailored to demystify the process, offering a step-by-step approach to mastering LBOs in today's dynamic global markets.

Copyright

Dedication

To the dealmakers, strategists, and financial innovators shaping the future of private equity. Your commitment to excellence and relentless pursuit of value inspires this work.

Acknowledgments

We extend our gratitude to the experts, mentors, and industry leaders who contributed to the insights and frameworks presented in this masterclass. Special thanks to the VCII community for fostering an environment of collaboration and continuous learning.

Why Choose VCII?

The Value Creation Innovation Institute (VCII) is at the forefront of private equity education, specializing in value creation and business transformation. The Advanced LBO Masterclass (ALBOM) is designed to provide participants with an unmatched learning experience tailored to the evolving demands of the industry.

What Sets VCII Apart?

1. **Specialized Focus on Value Creation:**
   - VCII's curriculum is meticulously designed to address the nuances of value creation in private equity. With an emphasis on practical application, participants are equipped to tackle real-world challenges.
2. **Nonprofit Commitment:**
   - As a nonprofit organization, VCII is dedicated to delivering high-quality education at accessible prices, making elite-level training affordable for professionals worldwide.
3. **Global Recognition:**
   - VCII certifications are respected by financial institutions, private equity firms, and global organizations. With participants from over 85 countries, the institute fosters a truly international community.

Why Take the Advanced LBO Masterclass?

The ALBOM offers a transformative learning experience that bridges foundational knowledge with advanced strategies. Here's why it stands out:

Comprehensive Curriculum:

- The course delves into every aspect of LBOs, from deal structuring and valuation to AI-driven innovations and crisis management. Participants gain a 360-degree understanding of the LBO process.

Practical Application:

- Real-world case studies and a capstone project enable participants to apply theoretical insights to practical scenarios, ensuring a seamless transition to workplace challenges.

Cutting-Edge Insights:

- With topics such as ESG integration, digital private equity, and AI-driven analytics, ALBOM prepares learners to excel in the future of private equity.

Flexible Learning Format:

- Designed for professionals, the course is delivered in modular format, allowing participants to progress at their own pace without compromising their work commitments.

Who Should Take This Course?

The Advanced LBO Masterclass caters to professionals at various career stages, providing tailored insights and tools to advance their expertise in private equity.

1. **Early-Career Professionals:**
    - Aspiring private equity analysts and associates.
    - Recent graduates preparing for roles in financial services.
2. **Mid-Career Professionals:**
    - Managers and consultants transitioning into private equity.
    - Operating partners seeking deeper knowledge of LBO strategies.
3. **Senior Executives and Leadership:**
    - CEOs, CFOs, and portfolio company leaders aligning with private equity objectives.
    - Industry veterans aiming to refine strategic and operational expertise.
4. **Financial Strategists:**
    - Advisors and fund managers supporting private equity investments.
    - Professionals overseeing institutional portfolios with a private equity focus.

Learning Objectives

By the end of the Advanced LBO Masterclass, participants will:

1. **Master the Fundamentals of LBOs:**
   - Understand the lifecycle of leveraged buyouts, including structuring, financing, and stakeholder alignment.
2. **Develop Advanced Deal-Making Expertise:**
   - Gain insights into sourcing, evaluating, and executing deals with precision.
   - Learn to negotiate terms, manage covenants, and ensure post-deal integration success.
3. **Leverage Cutting-Edge Tools:**
   - Explore the role of AI, blockchain, and data analytics in transforming LBO strategies.
   - Integrate ESG factors into deal assessments to align with modern investment priorities.
4. **Enhance Value Creation Capabilities:**
   - Identify operational inefficiencies, drive cost reductions, and implement strategic growth initiatives in portfolio companies.
5. **Prepare for Future Trends:**
   - Understand the implications of emerging markets, decentralized finance, and technological disruption on private equity.
6. **Apply Knowledge Practically:**
   - Participate in real-world case studies, scenario analyses, and a capstone project that mirrors private equity challenges.

The ALBOM Advantage

Expert Instruction:

- The course is delivered by seasoned private equity professionals, thought leaders, and academic experts, ensuring a blend of theoretical depth and practical relevance.

Global Community:

- Join a network of like-minded professionals and industry leaders, fostering collaboration and shared learning across borders.

Career Advancement:

- Gain the skills and credentials to excel in private equity, with opportunities for leadership roles, promotions, and impactful contributions to the field.

Course Structure

The Advanced LBO Masterclass is divided into key modules, each designed to build a strong foundation and advance into specialized topics. Modules include:

1. **Introduction to LBOs:** History, key concepts, and market impact.
2. **Valuation and Financial Modeling:** Practical tools for accurate deal evaluation.
3. **Negotiation and Deal Structuring:** Strategies for securing optimal terms.
4. **Operational Excellence:** Driving value creation in portfolio companies.
5. **Exit Strategies:** Traditional and innovative approaches to maximizing returns.
6. **Emerging Trends:** ESG, AI, and technological advancements shaping the future of LBOs.

How to Use This Book

The *Advanced LBO Masterclass* is divided into structured lessons, each focusing on critical components of LBOs—from valuation and financial modeling to crisis management and innovative exit strategies. Each lesson is supported by:

1. **Objectives:** Clear goals for knowledge acquisition and skill development.
2. **Content:** Detailed explanations, practical examples, and case studies.
3. **Takeaways:** Key insights for quick reference.
4. **Self-Study Questions:** Prompts to reinforce learning and encourage application.
5. **References:** Additional resources for deeper exploration.

Whether you are a seasoned private equity professional or a newcomer to the field, this book is designed to guide your journey through the intricate and rewarding world of LBOs.

Enroll in the Advanced LBO Masterclass today and take the next step in mastering the art and science of leveraged buyouts. Together, let's shape the future of private equity.

Lesson 1: Introduction to Leveraged Buyouts

Lesson Objectives

By the end of this lesson, participants will be able to:

1. **Define leveraged buyouts (LBOs) and understand their core mechanics.**
2. **Differentiate LBOs** from other corporate finance strategies such as mergers, acquisitions, and venture capital.
3. **Trace the evolution of LBOs** from historical milestones to present-day practices.
4. **Analyze the relevance and application of LBOs** in today's global financial markets.

What Are Leveraged Buyouts?

Leveraged buyouts (LBOs) involve acquiring companies using significant borrowed funds. This minimizes equity contribution while maintaining control.

Collateral

Acquired company's assets and cash flows secure the loans.

Value Creation

Effective LBOs rely on operational improvements and financial restructuring.

Strategy

Strategic repositioning maximizes value in leveraged buyouts.

Lesson Content

1. Definitions and Core Concepts

A **leveraged buyout (LBO)** is a financial transaction in which an investor or group of investors—most commonly a private equity (PE) firm—acquires a target company by using a significant amount of borrowed funds. The acquired company's assets and future cash flows typically serve as collateral for these loans. By employing a high degree of leverage, the acquirer can minimize its equity contribution while still maintaining control of the business.

1.1 Why Use Leverage?

Leverage magnifies potential returns. When a deal goes well—meaning the acquired company's cash flows grow and the debt is serviced effectively—the equity owners can achieve **outsized returns**. However, this strategy also amplifies risk; if the company underperforms, the heavy debt burden can lead to defaults, restructurings, or even bankruptcy.

In essence, LBOs are about **maximizing value creation** through operational improvements, financial restructuring, and strategic repositioning. Private equity firms seek to exit these investments—often after three to seven years—via an initial public offering (IPO), a sale to a strategic buyer, or a secondary buyout to another PE firm.

Key Takeaway: The primary appeal of LBOs is the potential for large gains through relatively small equity investments, but the high leverage can quickly become a liability if market conditions or internal operations deteriorate.

1.2 Key Features of LBOs

1. **High Leverage**
   Debt can account for anywhere between **50% and 90%** of the acquisition price. The exact structure might include senior secured loans (first lien), subordinated or mezzanine financing, and possibly bonds or other debt instruments, depending on market conditions and the target's credit quality.

2. **Ownership Transfer**
   Post-acquisition, the buying entity—often a PE sponsor—assumes majority ownership. They typically install new management or work closely with existing leadership to implement strategy shifts and drive post-deal value creation.

3. **Risk-Reward Dynamics**
   Because leverage amplifies returns, a small equity stake can turn into substantial profits

upon a successful exit. Conversely, underperformance can lead to ballooning interest expenses and possible default.

4. **Focus on Cash Flow**
   LBOs fundamentally rely on the target's ability to generate enough cash flow to meet interest and principal repayments. Companies with stable, recurring revenues are prime candidates for LBO transactions.

5. **Operational Improvements**
   LBOs are not purely about financial engineering. Effective sponsors often employ a hands-on approach—improving supply chain efficiencies, cutting redundant costs, and enhancing product lines—to boost EBITDA and drive long-term growth.

Why Use Leverage?

Amplified Returns

Leverage enables large acquisitions with minimal equity, potentially yielding outsized profits.

Growth Potential

Successful LBOs can lead to significant cash flow growth and debt repayment.

Risk Amplification

Leverage also increases risk, requiring careful planning to avoid financial distress.

Strategic Planning

Careful management is crucial to prevent defaults, restructurings, or bankruptcies.

2. A Hypothetical Manufacturing LBO Example

To illustrate the mechanics of an LBO, consider a manufacturing firm valued at **$1 billion**. Assume it generates **$100 million** in EBITDA (Earnings Before Interest, Taxes, Depreciation, and Amortization):

- **Purchase Price**: $800 million (applying an 8x EBITDA multiple).
- **Financing Structure**:
    - **Senior Debt**: $400 million
    - **Mezzanine Debt**: $200 million
    - **Equity**: $200 million
- **Leverage Ratio**: 75% debt, 25% equity

In this scenario, the total purchase price is $800 million, of which $600 million is financed by debt. The remaining $200 million represents the PE sponsor's equity contribution. Over the holding period, the sponsor will aim to grow EBITDA—perhaps from $100 million to $120 million or more—while paying down a portion of the debt. Upon exit, if the sponsor sells the company at a similar or higher multiple, the **equity portion** could be worth significantly more than $200 million, resulting in a strong internal rate of return (IRR).

Practical Insight: Even modest improvements in EBITDA can translate into large gains for equity holders because the debt portion remains fixed (aside from principal repayments). This is one reason sponsors emphasize operational excellence and financial discipline in LBO transactions.

Operational Improvements in Practice

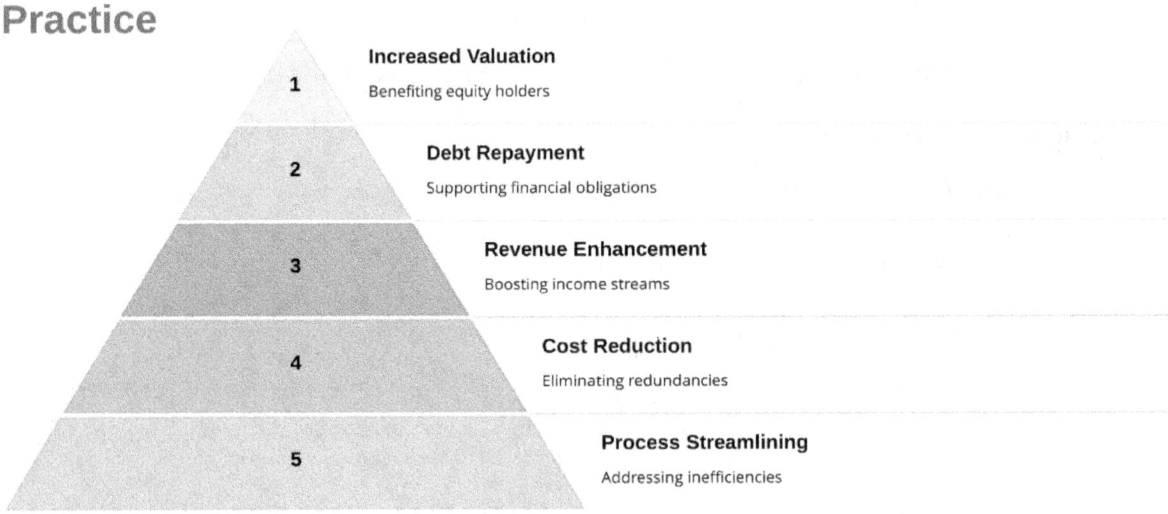

Operational improvements are crucial for LBO success. They unlock growth potential and increase company valuation, ultimately benefiting equity holders.

3. Historical Milestones of LBOs

The development of LBOs over the past several decades reflects how market conditions, regulatory changes, and financial innovations intersect to reshape the landscape of corporate finance.

3.1 The 1980s: Junk Bonds and the Rise of Modern LBOs

- **High-Yield Financing**: The widespread use of junk bonds—championed by Michael Milken at Drexel Burnham Lambert—gave acquirers unprecedented access to capital for large-scale buyouts.
- **Iconic Deal: RJR Nabisco (1988)**: Acquired by Kohlberg Kravis Roberts (KKR) for $25 billion, this transaction became synonymous with the era's financial excess and creativity. Chronicled in *Barbarians at the Gate*, it showcased both the potential profits and the reputational risks tied to LBOs.
- **Regulatory Backlash**: Several leveraged companies fell into distress, prompting criticism that such deals were fueling corporate instability. This led to increased scrutiny and discussions about more stringent regulations.

3.2 The 1990s: Slowdown, Consolidation, and Rebound

- **Early 1990s Recession**: A sluggish economy and higher interest rates dampened appetite for highly leveraged transactions.
- **Shift in Strategy**: Private equity firms recognized that pure financial engineering was insufficient. They began focusing more on **operational turnarounds**, investing in processes and people to stabilize and grow portfolio companies.
- **Renewed Growth**: As the economy recovered in the mid-to-late 1990s, PE firms regained momentum, supported by rising equity markets and investor confidence.

3.3 The 2000s: Mega-Deals, Globalization, and the Financial Crisis

- **Mega-LBOs**: Transactions like the $44 billion buyout of TXU Energy, and Blackstone's $26 billion acquisition of Hilton Hotels, demonstrated the colossal scale possible in a frothy credit environment.
- **International Expansion**: Private equity capital flowed into Asia, Latin America, and Eastern Europe. Investors sought higher-growth economies with less competitive deal processes.
- **Financial Crisis (2008)**: The collapse of credit markets abruptly halted large-scale LBO deals. Many existing leveraged companies had to refinance, restructure, or negotiate covenant waivers, illustrating the inherent perils of high leverage in a downturn.

3.4 Post-2010: Innovation, ESG Integration, and Technological Edge

- **Financing Innovations**: The rise of **unitranche debt**—combining senior and subordinated debt into a single facility—offered more flexible funding. **Covenant-lite loans** reduced lenders' protections, granting borrowers additional freedom in managing operations.
- **ESG and Sustainability**: Growing focus on **environmental, social, and governance (ESG)** metrics shaped investment committees' decisions. Investors began demanding greater accountability and socially responsible strategies.
- **Technology-Driven Value Creation**: Sophisticated analytics, digital transformation roadmaps, and AI-driven insights emerged as new levers for improving operations and identifying synergies.

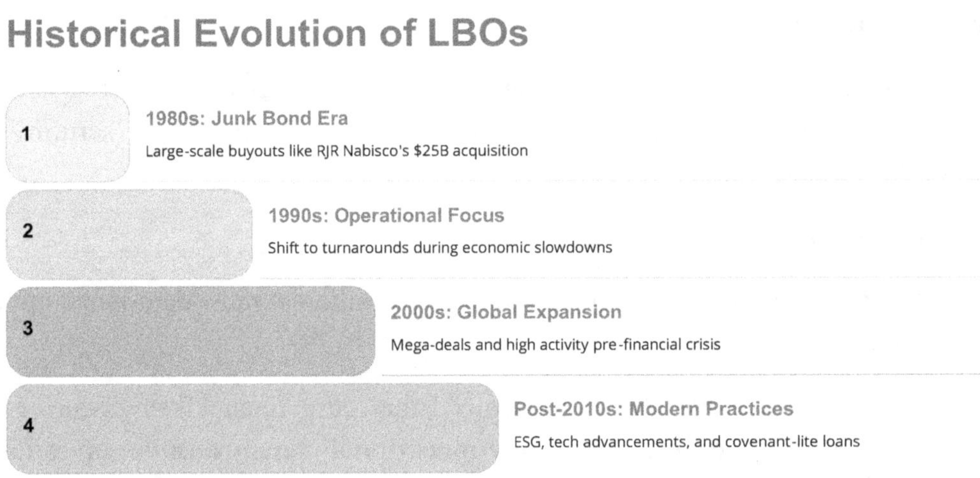

LBOs have transformed over decades, adapting to economic conditions and market trends. Each era brought unique characteristic s, shaping the LBO landscape we see today.

Exhibit 1: Key LBO Milestones

- **1988**: RJR Nabisco buyout (~$25 billion) becomes a symbol of LBO era.
- **2007**: TXU Energy buyout (~$44 billion) highlights the heights of mega-LBOs.
- **2008**: Financial crisis severely hampers leveraged financing.
- **2018 onwards**: ESG, data analytics, and covenant-lite structures dominate modern PE deals.

4. Differentiating LBOs from Other Strategies

While LBOs are a prominent feature of corporate finance, they differ in distinct ways from **mergers and acquisitions (M&A)**, **venture capital (VC)**, and even standard corporate debt financing.

Feature	LBOs	M&A (Strategic)	Venture Capital (VC)
Primary Focus	Leverage-driven value creation	Synergies, market share, integration	Funding early-stage high-growth businesses
Ownership	Usually majority or full control	Varies (outright buy or partial stake)	Typically minority stakes in startups
Capital Structure	High ratio of debt to equity	Can be a mix of equity and debt	Primarily equity (seed, Series A, B, etc.)
Risk Profile	Elevated financial risk due to leverage	Moderate to high (depends on synergy)	High business model/market risk
Exit Horizon	3–7 years (IPO, sale, or recap).	No fixed horizon (depends on strategy)	Potentially 5–10 years or more

Example:

- In an **LBO**, a PE firm acquires a steady manufacturing company, optimizes production, and sells it for a profit within five years.
- In a **strategic M&A deal**, a competitor buys the same company to integrate its product lines and consolidate the market.
- In **venture capital**, an early-stage biotech startup receives funds to develop an unproven product, with minimal revenue but high potential.

Key Insight: LBOs target relatively mature businesses with predictable cash flows, while VC invests in companies with uncertain revenue trajectories but significant growth potential.

5. Relevance of LBOs in Today's Markets

Despite economic cycles and regulatory changes, LBOs remain a central pillar of private equity deal-making. Their adaptability is evident in how they align with global expansion, technological advancements, and shifting investor sentiments.

5.1 Globalization

- **Emerging Markets**: Firms seek out less-saturated regions where valuations might be lower and growth potential higher (e.g., Southeast Asia, parts of Africa).
- **Cross-Border Deals**: Large PE players are increasingly involved in multinational transactions, which require navigating complex legal, cultural, and regulatory environments.

5.2 Technological Advancements

- **Data-Driven Target Sourcing**: AI and machine learning help identify undervalued businesses or particular operational inefficiencies ripe for improvement.
- **Digital Transformation of Portfolio Companies**: Post-acquisition, PE sponsors often accelerate digital initiatives—implementing new CRM systems, automating manufacturing lines, or harnessing e-commerce channels to spur revenue growth.

5.3 ESG and Sustainability

- **Investor Pressure**: Limited partners (LPs) now place more weight on ESG factors, from carbon footprints to board diversity.
- **Long-Term Value**: Beyond compliance, adopting sustainable practices can enhance brand value, attract new customers, and even reduce costs (e.g., energy efficiencies).

Exhibit 2: Modern LBO Dimensions

- **Private Equity Focus**: Dominates global LBO activity, with specialized funds targeting healthcare, technology, real estate, and more.
- **Regulatory Trends**: Covenant-lite loans and flexible financing structures reflect a lenient lending environment, though looming interest rate changes can alter this landscape.
- **Technological Edge**: Advanced analytics enable better due diligence and facilitate granular tracking of operational key performance indicators (KPIs).
- **ESG Integration**: Drives strategic decision-making to ensure deals align with stakeholder expectations and responsible investing principles.

Self-Study Questions

1. **Define a leveraged buyout (LBO).** How does high leverage both increase returns and amplify risk?
2. **Contrast LBOs with mergers & acquisitions (M&A).** What are the strategic vs. financial incentives in each scenario?
3. **Discuss the historical evolution of LBOs.** How did the 1980s junk bond era shape modern leveraged finance practices?
4. **Why are stable cash flows critical** in evaluating a company for an LBO? Provide an example of how these cash flows support the deal's debt burden.
5. **How have ESG and technology** changed the way private equity firms approach LBO opportunities in recent years?

Differentiating LBOs from Other Strategies

Primary Focus

LBOs: Leverage-driven value creation

M&A: Synergies

VC: Early-stage funding

Ownership

LBOs: Majority control

M&A and VC: Varied ownership structures

Capital Structure

LBOs: High debt-to-equity ratios

M&A and VC: Balanced or equity-heavy funding

Lesson Takeaways

- **LBOs use significant debt financing** to acquire companies, relying on the target's own cash flows for debt service. This can yield substantial equity returns if properly executed, but also elevates financial risk.
- **Historical context is vital**: From the 1980s junk bond surge to post-2008 restructuring, LBOs have continually adapted to economic and regulatory environments.
- **Differentiation from other strategies** (like venture capital or strategic M&A) highlights the unique attributes of LBOs: shorter holding periods, emphasis on operational discipline, and reliance on leverage.
- **Globalization, ESG, and technology** currently shape the LBO landscape, driving new frontiers in value creation and risk management.
- **A balanced approach to operations and finances**—rather than purely financial engineering—has become the hallmark of the most successful LBOs in the modern era.

Global Relevance of LBOs

1. **Globalization**
   LBOs adapt to global markets, offering untapped opportunities in emerging economies.
2. **Technology**
   Advanced analytics and AI enhance precision in target sourcing and optimization.
3. **ESG Priorities**
   LBOs evolve to incorporate environmental, social, and governance considerations.

References and Further Reading

1. **Kaplan, S. N., & Strömberg, P. (2009).** *Leveraged Buyouts and Private Equity. Journal of Economic Perspectives*.
2. **Gaughan, P. A. (2017).** *Mergers, Acquisitions, and Corporate Restructurings*. Wiley.
3. **Rosenbaum, J., & Pearl, J. (2020).** *Investment Banking: Valuation, Leveraged Buyouts, and Mergers & Acquisitions*. Wiley.
4. **VCII Institute**: In-depth case studies on iconic LBOs, highlighting best practices and pitfalls in deal structuring.
5. **Burrough, B., & Helyar, J. (1990).** *Barbarians at the Gate: The Fall of RJR Nabisco.* A seminal narrative on the defining LBO of the 1980s.
6. **PRI (Principles for Responsible Investment)**: Updated resources and guidelines on integrating ESG into private equity strategies.

Lesson 2: LBO Mechanics and Structuring

Lesson Objectives

By the end of this lesson, participants will be able to:

1. **Identify the key stakeholders** in an LBO and understand their respective roles.
2. **Analyze the financial leverage and debt-equity mix** crucial to an LBO structure.
3. **Evaluate the characteristics of ideal LBO candidates**, including financial and operational considerations.
4. **Optimize capital structure** to balance risk, cost, and operational flexibility.

Key Stakeholders in LBOs

Sponsors

Private equity firms lead acquisition, driving operational improvements for profitable exit.

Lenders

Provide majority financing through layered debt structures, ensuring secure returns.

Target Management

Execute strategic changes using intimate business knowledge.

Advisors

Legal, financial, and operational experts ensure compliant, well-structured deals.

Lesson Content

1. Anatomy of an LBO

A **leveraged buyout (LBO)** is best viewed as a sophisticated financial ecosystem where each player—sponsors, lenders, target management, and various advisors—performs a distinct yet interdependent role. LBOs hinge on striking a careful balance between debt and equity to maximize value creation.

1.1 Key Stakeholders

1. **Sponsors**
   - Typically private equity (PE) firms, investment groups, or consortiums that originate and orchestrate the LBO.
   - Contribute the equity portion of the financing and oversee **post-acquisition** initiatives (e.g., cost optimization, strategic realignment).
   - Focus intently on boosting operational performance and expanding the target's market reach to create an attractive exit scenario (such as a sale or IPO).
   - Collaborate closely with lenders and management to ensure each party's incentives align, often structuring **equity incentive plans** for key executives.
2. **Lenders**
   - Provide the lion's share of the acquisition financing. This can include **commercial banks**, **mezzanine lenders**, and **high-yield bond investors**.
   - Craft loan terms and covenants to mitigate risk (e.g., requiring certain levels of leverage ratios or placing restrictions on dividend payments).
   - Conduct extensive due diligence to evaluate the target's cash flow stability and ascertain whether the projected EBITDA improvements are realistic.
   - Frequently demand board observation rights or reporting requirements to monitor the financial health of the company.
3. **Target Management**
   - Integral to operational success post-acquisition. They possess intimate knowledge of the company's daily processes, customer relations, and potential inefficiencies.
   - Often incentivized via equity stakes, performance-based bonuses, or profit-sharing plans, ensuring that management remains dedicated to driving profitability.

- Key to identifying and implementing strategic initiatives—such as cost-cutting, pricing adjustments, and product/market expansion.

4. **Advisors**
    - **Investment bankers** facilitate deal negotiations, help structure the financing, and may also assist in raising debt or equity.
    - **Legal advisors** ensure compliance with securities laws, draft transaction documents, and handle regulatory filings.
    - **Consultants** (strategy, operations, HR, IT) may be brought in to perform detailed operational audits or to streamline post-acquisition integration efforts.
    - **Accounting firms** often conduct financial diligence (Quality of Earnings reports) to validate the target's historical and projected cash flows.

Key Insight: An LBO's success relies on well-coordinated stakeholder collaboration. Each stakeholder has specific incentives, but synergy among them is what fosters the operational and financial improvements that drive profitable exits.

Lenders and Their Financing Approach

Senior Debt
Secured against assets. Lower interest rates but strict covenants.

Mezzanine Debt
Bridges financing gap. Higher returns for increased risk.

High-Yield Bonds
Adds flexibility at higher cost. Less restrictive terms.

Risk Mitigation
Lenders rely on cash flow stability. May impose monitoring requirements.

2. Financial Leverage and the Debt-Equity Mix

At the heart of any LBO is **leverage**—the use of borrowed capital to increase potential returns on equity. This section explores the delicate equilibrium between debt (senior, mezzanine, high-yield) and equity contributions, emphasizing why free cash flow generation is paramount.

2.1 Debt Financing

- **Proportion of Financing**
  Debt often constitutes **50% to 90%** of the total transaction value. Deals on the higher end of that range carry substantial risk, as debt servicing can become onerous if market conditions sour or if projections fall short.

- **Layers of Debt**
  Most LBOs use a layered approach:

  1. **Senior Debt**: Typically secured by the target's assets (inventory, receivables, property, etc.). This debt has the lowest cost but tends to feature the most restrictive covenants.

  2. **Mezzanine Debt**: Subordinated to senior debt, commands higher interest rates, and sometimes includes features like **payment-in-kind (PIK)** interest or equity warrants.

  3. **High-Yield Bonds**: Often unsecured, carrying higher coupon rates. These bonds are popular in "mega-deals" where sponsors value flexibility and can tolerate higher interest costs.

- **Cash Flow Reliance**
  Because debt service (interest + principal repayment) depends on the target's operating cash flows, industries with **stable and predictable revenues** (e.g., consumer staples, utilities) are prime LBO candidates. Companies with volatile cash flows may still be targets if the sponsor believes it can significantly reduce variability or if the upside justifies the additional risk.

- **Covenants and Monitoring**
  Lenders impose financial covenants—such as maintaining a certain **interest coverage ratio** or not exceeding a set **total debt-to-EBITDA ratio**. Breach of these covenants can trigger default, forcing renegotiations or even leading to distressed asset sales.

2.2 Equity Financing

- **Equity Contribution**
  Sponsors usually invest **10% to 50%** of the transaction value. In extreme cases, the equity component may be smaller if the sponsor is highly confident in the target's stable cash flows or if the market for credit is particularly frothy.

- **"Skin in the Game"**
  Sponsors' equity acts as the cornerstone of deal credibility, aligning their fortunes with the success of the company. The more equity sponsors invest, the more confidence they signal to lenders and management that they're committed to a successful turnaround or growth strategy.

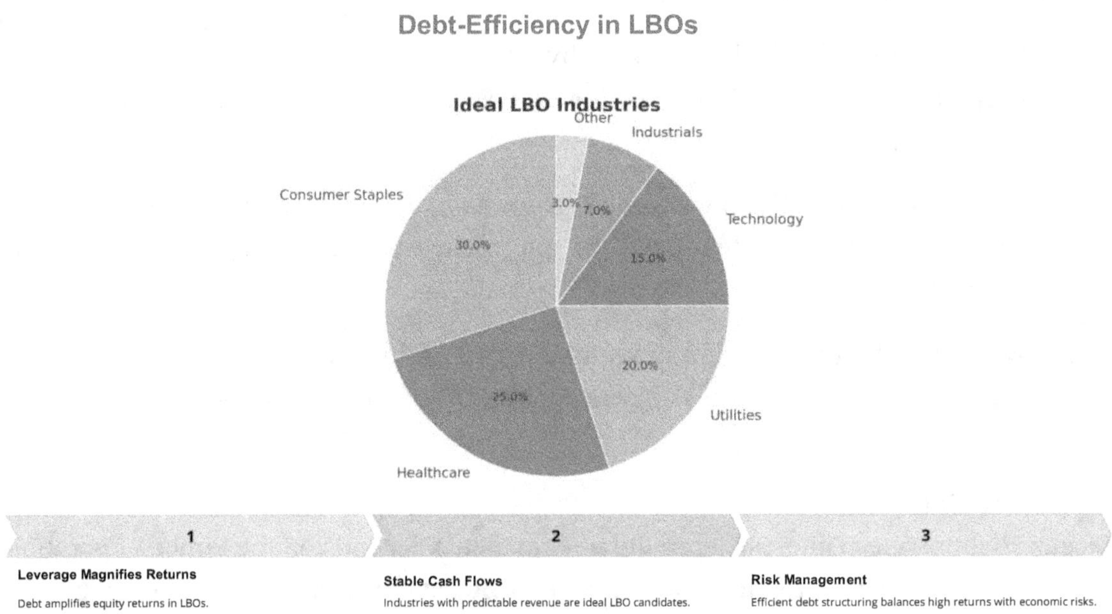

Example Financing Mix

- **Senior Debt**: 40–70% (Secured by the target's assets; lower interest rates, strict covenants)
- **Mezzanine Debt**: 10–20% (Higher rates, may include equity kickers)
- **High-Yield Bonds**: 10–30% (Unsecured, flexible terms, higher coupons)
- **Equity**: 10–50% (Provided by the sponsors; highest risk-reward)

3. Candidate Characteristics

Selecting the right target is often half the battle in orchestrating a successful LBO. Financial and operational attributes must align with the sponsors' strategic objectives and risk tolerance.

3.1 Financial Attributes

1. **Predictable Cash Flows**
    - Stability is essential for servicing significant debt obligations.
    - Companies in sectors like **healthcare, utilities, or consumer non-discretionary** goods often have more reliable streams of income.
    - Predictable revenue reduces default risk and provides lenders with reassurance.
2. **Strong Asset Base**
    - Tangible assets (e.g., machinery, real estate) can serve as collateral, improving borrowing capacity.
    - Intangibles (brands, patents) can bolster valuations but may require lenders specialized in intellectual property financing.
    - A strong asset foundation helps secure more favorable interest rates or larger credit lines.
3. **Low Existing Leverage**
    - The target's current debt level affects how much additional leverage can be introduced without pushing the company into dangerous territory.
    - Companies with minimal balance sheet debt have a **"clean slate"** for sponsors to layer on new debt financing to fund the acquisition.

Ideal LBO Candidate Characteristics

Strong Cash Flow

Consistent, predictable cash flow is crucial for servicing debt and supporting operations.

Low Existing Leverage

Minimal pre-existing debt allows for more flexibility in structuring the buyout.

Operational Inefficiencies

Opportunities for improvement can lead to increased value and profitability post-acquisition.

Stable Industry

Sectors like healthcare or utilities offer predictable revenue streams.

Strong asset base and identifiable growth opportunities enhance borrowing capacity and attractiveness.

Equity's Role in LBO Financing

1. **Equity Contribution**

   Typical sponsor investment range in transaction value

2. **Confidence Signal**

   Equity serves as a buffer for lenders

3. **Key Objectives**

   Drive EBITDA growth and strategic improvements

A well-balanced equity contribution builds credibility, attracting favorable debt terms. It increases the likelihood of achieving projected returns during the holding period.

3.2 Operational Attributes

1. **Market Positioning**
   - Established players with **strong brand recognition** or large market shares enjoy competitive advantages—often translating into sustained cash flows.
   - Defensive industries (e.g., waste management, consumer staples) tend to weather economic downturns better.
   - Growth markets or niche segments also attract PE sponsors looking for upside potential.
2. **Improvement Potential**
   - Targets with known inefficiencies (outdated systems, excess overhead, poor supply chain management) can see a **boost in profitability** once these issues are fixed.
   - Synergies may exist if the PE sponsor already owns portfolio companies in the same or complementary sectors—allowing knowledge transfers, shared distribution, or cross-selling.

Case Example

- **Company X**: A mid-sized consumer goods manufacturer posting $50 million annual EBITDA, with **60% gross margins** and **under-leveraged** balance sheet.
  - **Predictable Cash Flows**: Loyal customer base and recurring sales contracts.
  - **Tangible Assets**: $200 million worth of manufacturing equipment and real estate.
  - **Improvement Potential**: Supply chain inefficiencies, which if optimized, could reduce costs and increase EBITDA to $60–$65 million.

4. Capital Structure Optimization

Designing the right capital structure is akin to assembling a puzzle: each layer of debt and equity must fit cohesively to support the target's operations and growth while minimizing the overall cost of capital.

4.1 Debt Layers

1. **Senior Debt**
   - Secured by the target's assets, offering lenders more security and thus lower interest rates.
   - Typically structured as **term loans** (Term Loan A or B) and revolving credit facilities for working capital.
   - Comes with **restrictive covenants** (e.g., maximum leverage ratio), limiting management's strategic freedom.
2. **Mezzanine Debt**
   - Occupies the middle ground between senior debt and equity.
   - Commands higher returns, often featuring equity-like instruments (warrants) or PIK interest options.
   - Useful when sponsors wish to reduce pure equity contribution but can't (or won't) secure additional senior debt.
3. **High-Yield Bonds**
   - Unsecured debt with higher coupon rates.
   - Used in larger or more complex LBOs where sponsors need flexibility and can stomach bigger interest expenses.
   - Often provides fewer operational covenants, granting management more freedom than strict bank loans.

4.2 Role of Risk Transfer

Modern LBOs may incorporate **securitization** or **syndication** to spread risk and attract a wider pool of investors:

- **Securitization**: Bundles the LBO debt (or specific receivables) into marketable securities, which are then sold to institutional investors.
- **Syndicated Loans**: Multiple banks or financial institutions jointly provide large credit facilities, reducing individual lender exposure.

Case Example: Optimized Structure

- **Target Company**: A $1 billion retailer producing $150 million in EBITDA.
- **Proposed Capital Structure**:
    - $500 million Senior Debt (secured by inventory and real estate).
    - $200 million Mezzanine Debt (second lien on assets, higher interest rate).
    - $100 million High-Yield Bonds (unsecured, flexible terms).
    - $200 million Sponsor Equity.
- **Rationale**: This blend balances lower-cost senior debt with the flexibility of high-yield bonds, while not overburdening the sponsor's equity commitment.

5. Stress Testing and Scenario Analysis

No capital structure is complete without evaluating how the target would fare under **various economic and operational scenarios**. Stress tests help sponsors and lenders understand the margin of safety:

1. **Base Case**
    - Assumes moderate growth, stable interest rates, and predictable EBITDA.
    - Typically forms the foundation of the deal's valuation and pro forma financials.
2. **Recession/Downturn Case**
    - Models severe revenue declines or margin compressions to determine if the company can still **service its debt**.
    - Examines worst-case scenarios for covenant breaches or potential restructuring.
3. **Growth/Best Case**
    - Considers favorable market conditions, successful operational improvements, and above-average revenue expansion.
    - Reveals how quickly debt could be repaid or refinanced at lower interest rates, and how equity values might scale up.

Key Ratios in Stress Testing

- **Debt Service Coverage Ratio (DSCR)**: Measures the company's ability to cover debt payments with net operating income.
- **Loan-to-Value (LTV) Ratio**: Compares the outstanding debt to the fair market value of the assets (or enterprise value).
- **Interest Coverage Ratio**: EBITDA (or EBIT) divided by interest expense; a lower ratio increases default risk.

Scenario	DSCR	Outcome
Base Case	2.5x	Healthy coverage; minimal risk of default
Recession Case	1.2x	Tight margins; requires focus on cost control
Growth/Best Case	3.0x	Ample coverage; potential for early debt prepayment

Self-Study Questions

1. **Identify the key stakeholders in an LBO** and explain how each contributes to the transaction's success or failure.
2. **Why are predictable cash flows so critical** for LBO success? Provide an example of a high-risk, low-stability target that might not be suitable for an LBO.
3. **Compare and contrast senior debt, mezzanine debt, and high-yield bonds** in an LBO structure. What trade-offs do sponsors face when selecting each layer?
4. **Discuss how stress testing and scenario analysis** bolster the robustness of an LBO's capital structure. Which ratios are most informative in gauging debt sustainability?
5. **Create a hypothetical LBO structure** for a $500 million revenue company with $50 million EBITDA. Justify your financing mix, explaining why you chose each debt instrument and the equity proportion.

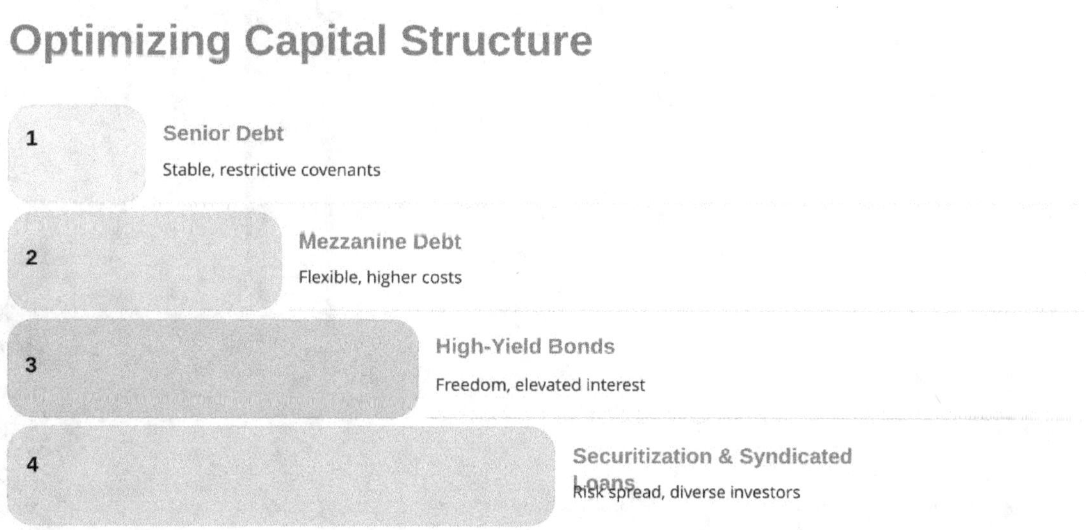

LBO capital structure balances debt and equity to minimize costs while supporting growth. Each debt type offers unique benefits and trade-offs. Securitization and syndicated loans ensure long-term sustainability by attracting diverse investors.

Lesson Takeaways

1. **Complex Stakeholder Ecosystem**: Successful LBOs require well-aligned incentives among sponsors, lenders, management, and advisors.
2. **Debt-Equity Mix**: Achieving the right blend of high-leverage potential and manageable risk hinges on understanding cash flow stability, collateral, and financing options.
3. **Ideal Candidates**: Predictable cash flows, a strong asset base, and clear operational upside are the hallmarks of prime LBO targets.
4. **Capital Structure Optimization**: Balancing cost of capital, covenant flexibility, and downside protection is critical. Tools like senior debt, mezzanine financing, and high-yield bonds each carry distinct benefits and risks.
5. **Stress Testing**: Rigorous scenario analyses ensure that the chosen structure can withstand economic headwinds and remain financially viable, protecting both lenders and equity investors.

Stress Testing Scenarios

1 **Base-Case**
Assumes moderate growth and stable interest rates.

2 **Recession Case**
Tests resilience under revenue declines.

3 **Best-Case**
Explores upside potential of market growth and operational success.

4 **Financial Ratios**
DSCR, LTV, and interest coverage assess financial health and risk.

References and Further Reading

1. **Rosenbaum, J., & Pearl, J. (2020).** *Investment Banking: Valuation, Leveraged Buyouts, and Mergers & Acquisitions.* Wiley.

2. **Damodaran, A. (2012).** *Investment Valuation: Tools and Techniques for Determining the Value of Any Asset.* Wiley.

3. **Kaplan, S. N., & Strömberg, P. (2009).** *Leveraged Buyouts and Private Equity. Journal of Economic Perspectives.*

4. Case Studies on Successful and Failed LBOs from **VCII Institute**—exploring different sectors and deal sizes.

5. Select articles on modern financing trends (e.g., covenant-lite, unitranche) from private equity publications such as **Private Equity International** or **Institutional Investor**.

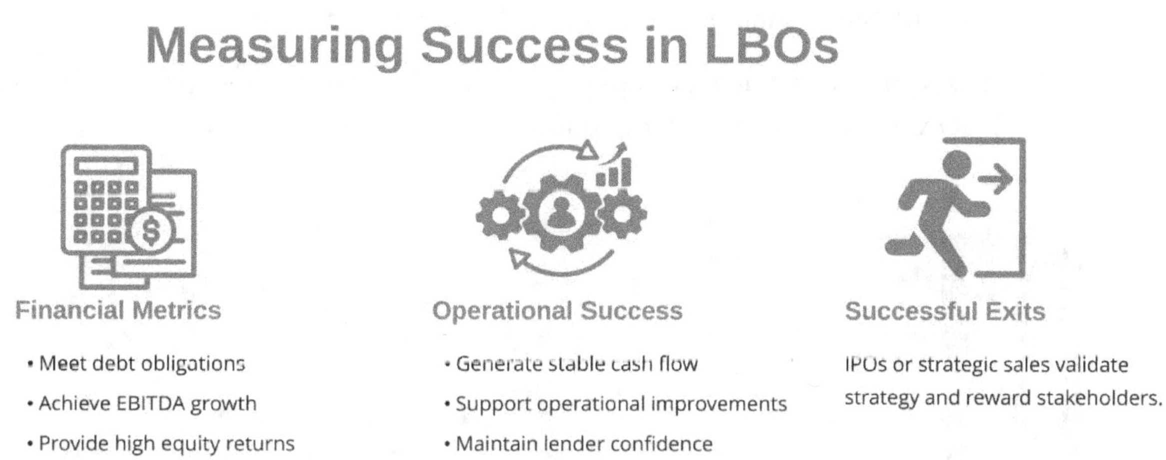

Lesson 3: Valuation and Modeling Techniques

Lesson Objectives

By the end of this lesson, participants will be able to:

1. **Understand the core valuation metrics** used in LBO transactions and their specific applications.
2. **Build a comprehensive LBO model**, including key input assumptions, multi-year projections, and an analysis of potential returns.
3. **Evaluate the impact of sensitivity and scenario analyses** on LBO outcomes, identifying how different assumptions can shift risk and return profiles.
4. **Integrate advanced techniques**, such as ESG metrics and real-time adjustments, into LBO valuations for a modern, robust approach.

Core Valuation Metrics

Enterprise Value (EV)

Measures total company value, including equity and debt.

EBITDA Multiples

Compares company value to earnings before interest, taxes, depreciation, and amortization.

Discounted Cash Flow

Estimates present value of future cash flows.

Market Comparables

Identifies valuation norms within a specific sector.

These metrics form the foundation for LBO valuations, helping assess pricing and align with return thresholds.

Lesson Content

1. Fundamental Valuation Metrics

Valuation sits at the epicenter of every leveraged buyout (LBO), guiding sponsors in determining an appropriate purchase price and ensuring the investment aligns with their desired return profile. While many valuation tools exist, three foundational methods—**Enterprise Value (EV)**, **EBITDA multiples**, and **Discounted Cash Flow (DCF)**—generally dominate LBO analysis.

1.1 Enterprise Value (EV)

Enterprise Value (EV) represents the total value of a company by combining its market capitalization and net debt (total debt minus cash). EV effectively captures the value "owed" to both equity holders and debt holders, making it a crucial metric in LBOs.

- **Why It Matters**
    1. **Debt-Neutral Comparison**: EV levels the playing field by reflecting a firm's value independent of its capital structure. Two companies with identical market caps but different debt levels may have very different EVs.
    2. **Foundation for Feasibility**: Sponsors use EV to assess whether the proposed transaction price aligns with their risk/return thresholds.
    3. **Basis for Multiples**: EV is often paired with EBITDA (or other operating metrics) to derive multiples that guide both entry and exit pricing in LBOs.

Quick Example

- Market Capitalization: $800 million
- Total Debt: $200 million
- Cash: $50 million
- **EV = $800 million + $200 million – $50 million = $950 million**

This $950 million often serves as a starting point in determining whether the acquisition is priced favorably relative to the company's earnings potential.

1.2 EBITDA Multiples

EBITDA (Earnings Before Interest, Taxes, Depreciation, and Amortization) approximates operating cash flow, making it particularly relevant for LBO deals where free cash flow must service significant debt.

- **Industry Norms**: Different sectors command different multiples based on growth potential, cyclicality, and competitive dynamics. For example, a high-growth tech firm could be valued at 10x or more of EBITDA, whereas a mature manufacturing company might trade at 6x.
- **Peer Comparisons**: Sponsors look at peers' valuation multiples to ascertain whether the target is overpriced or undervalued. They also adjust for company-specific factors like brand strength, customer concentration, and geographic diversification.
- **Synergy Premiums**: If a sponsor anticipates meaningful cost savings or revenue synergies, they may justify paying a slightly higher EBITDA multiple, confident that improved cash flows will balance out a higher purchase price.

Quick Example

- Target's EBITDA: $100 million
- Sector Multiple: 8x EBITDA
- **Valuation = $100 million x 8 = $800 million**

This method provides a **quick** and **transparent** way to triangulate a target's valuation, though sponsors often refine it with more granular analysis.

1.3 Discounted Cash Flow (DCF)

DCF is a more detailed method that calculates a firm's intrinsic value by forecasting future free cash flows (FCF) and discounting them back to present value using an appropriate discount rate (usually the **Weighted Average Cost of Capital, WACC**).

Key Steps

1. **Project Cash Flows**: Estimate revenues, costs, and capital expenditures (CapEx) over a 5- to 10-year horizon, arriving at yearly free cash flow figures.
2. **Determine Terminal Value**
    - **Perpetuity Growth Method**: Assumes cash flows continue growing at a modest perpetual rate (g).
    - **Exit Multiple Method**: Applies a future EV/EBITDA multiple to the final year's EBITDA.
3. **Discount Cash Flows**: The projected cash flows and terminal value are discounted back using WACC. A higher WACC indicates higher perceived risk, reducing present value.

Quick Example

- Projected Year-5 FCF: $50 million
- Terminal Growth Rate (g): 2%
- WACC (r): 10%

Sponsors calculate the terminal value, discount it to present, and then sum all discounted cash flows. This holistic approach is particularly valuable for targets in **fast-changing industries** or where sponsors expect **significant operational improvements**.

2. Sensitivity and Scenario Analysis

No valuation model is complete without examining how **key assumptions** might shift in various market conditions. **Sensitivity** and **scenario** analyses serve as reality checks, revealing where risks might lie if conditions differ from initial forecasts.

2.1 Sensitivity Analysis

Sensitivity analysis involves tweaking one input at a time—such as revenue growth, EBITDA margins, WACC, or exit multiples—to see how the valuation (or returns) respond.

- **Revenue Growth**: If growth falls from 5% to 3%, the future cash flows drop, lowering both DCF-based valuations and IRRs.
- **EBITDA Margins**: Even a few percentage points' difference in margins can significantly impact free cash flow, especially when leverage is high.
- **WACC**: A higher discount rate reduces present value, reflecting increased risk or changing macroeconomic conditions (e.g., rising interest rates).
- **Exit Multiples**: If you plan to exit at an 8x multiple but the actual market multiple is 6x, the valuation—and thus equity returns—can deteriorate quickly.

Example

- A 1% change in EBITDA margin might swing the internal rate of return (IRR) by 2–3 percentage points, showing how crucial operational efficiency can be in a leveraged scenario.

2.2 Scenario Analysis

Scenario analysis changes **multiple inputs simultaneously**, reflecting different market or operational realities (e.g., baseline, downside, upside).

Scenario	Revenue Growth	EBITDA Margin	Valuation (M)
Base Case	5%	20%	$800
Recession Case	2%	15%	$650
Optimistic Case	8%	25%	$950

- **Base Case**: Reflects management's most likely forecast.
- **Recession Case**: Includes slower growth, higher costs, or margin compression. This helps sponsors test covenant headroom and debt service viability.
- **Optimistic Case**: Assumes robust demand and stronger margin execution. While often less probable, it shows the potential upside if conditions align favorably.

Key Takeaway: Sponsors rely on these scenarios to gauge resilience. If the LBO cannot withstand a mild downturn without breaching covenants, it may signal an overly aggressive capital structure or overpayment risk.

3. Building an LBO Model

A **well-structured LBO model** is the backbone of investment decisions, enabling sponsors to assess feasibility, returns, and risk levels in a systematic manner.

3.1 Step-by-Step Model Construction

1. **Input Assumptions**
   - **Purchase Price**: Often determined by a chosen EV/EBITDA multiple or a DCF-derived value.
   - **Financing Structure**: Breakdown of senior debt, mezzanine debt, high-yield bonds, and equity. Also include interest rates, covenants, and repayment schedules.
   - **Operating Assumptions**: Revenue growth, cost of goods sold (COGS), and SG&A expenses. Make sure to incorporate expected operational improvements or cost synergies.
2. **Sources and Uses Table**
   This table outlines how the deal is financed (Sources) and where the capital is allocated (Uses).

Example

Sources	Amount ($M)	Uses	Amount ($M)
Senior Debt	400	Purchase Price	700
Mezzanine Debt	200	Transaction Fees	20
Sponsor Equity	100	Working Capital	80
Total	700	**Total**	700

3. **Financial Projections**
   - Build out **Income Statement, Balance Sheet, and Cash Flow** forecasts over 5 to 10 years.
   - Factor in **operational shifts**: e.g., new product launches, efficiency gains, or changes in pricing strategy.

- Monitor changes in net working capital (NWC) to capture real-time liquidity impacts.

4. **Debt Schedule**
   - Detail each tranche of debt: principal amounts, interest rates, amortization profiles, and financial covenants.
   - Model potential refinancings or bullet maturities, including penalty fees if the sponsor opts for early repayments.
5. **Returns Calculation**
   - **Internal Rate of Return (IRR)**: Annualized rate reflecting the value sponsors expect to earn on their initial equity investment.
   - **Cash-on-Cash Multiple**: Summarizes total cash inflows (distributions, exit proceeds) over total equity contributed.
   - Sponsors often target IRRs above 20% (though this varies by region and risk profile).

Key Insight: A robust LBO model includes toggles for sensitivity/scenario analyses, ensuring sponsors can stress-test the deal's viability under shifting market conditions.

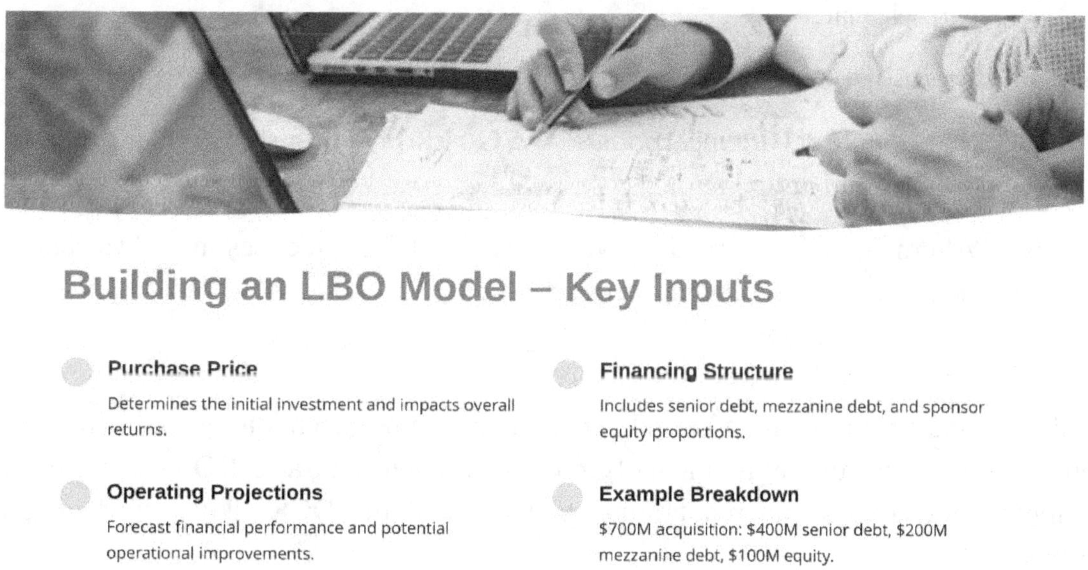

4. Advanced Techniques

As the private equity landscape evolves, **advanced modeling techniques** and **non-traditional considerations**—from ESG to real-time data integration—have become pivotal in modern LBO analyses.

4.1 Incorporating ESG Metrics

Environmental, Social, and Governance (ESG) factors now play a larger role in shaping valuations and lender/sponsor expectations.

1. **Impact on Cash Flows**
   - Sustainability initiatives (e.g., energy-efficient machinery, waste reduction) can lower long-term operating costs.
   - Strong social policies (e.g., fair labor practices) may boost brand value and customer loyalty, translating to higher revenue.
2. **Risk Mitigation**
   - ESG compliance can diminish risks of regulatory fines or reputational damage.
   - Identifying "brown" or socially contentious areas pre-acquisition can prevent costly surprises later.
3. **Valuation Adjustment**
   - Some sponsors are incorporating **ESG risk premiums** or discount rates to reflect reputational or operational risks.
   - Alternatively, a company with superior ESG practices may warrant a lower discount rate, recognizing reduced risk.

Example:

A chemical manufacturing target invests in carbon capture technology, reducing its carbon footprint and appealing to environmentally conscious clients. In an LBO context, the sponsor factors these cost savings and reputational benefits into the DCF, likely improving its IRR projections.

4.2 Stress Testing Models

Beyond standard scenario analyses, **stress testing** helps gauge the model's resilience under extreme conditions—an economic shock, sudden regulatory changes, or a collapse in consumer demand.

Scenario	Key Assumptions	Outcome
Base Case	Normal revenue & EBITDA	Covenants remain healthy
Downside Case	15% revenue decline, cost overruns	Possible covenant breach, restructuring
Upside Case	Above-average growth, margin expansion	Potential for early debt repayment

- **Stress testing** might include additional "what-if" conditions: interest rates spike by 200 basis points, or the target's largest customer leaves.

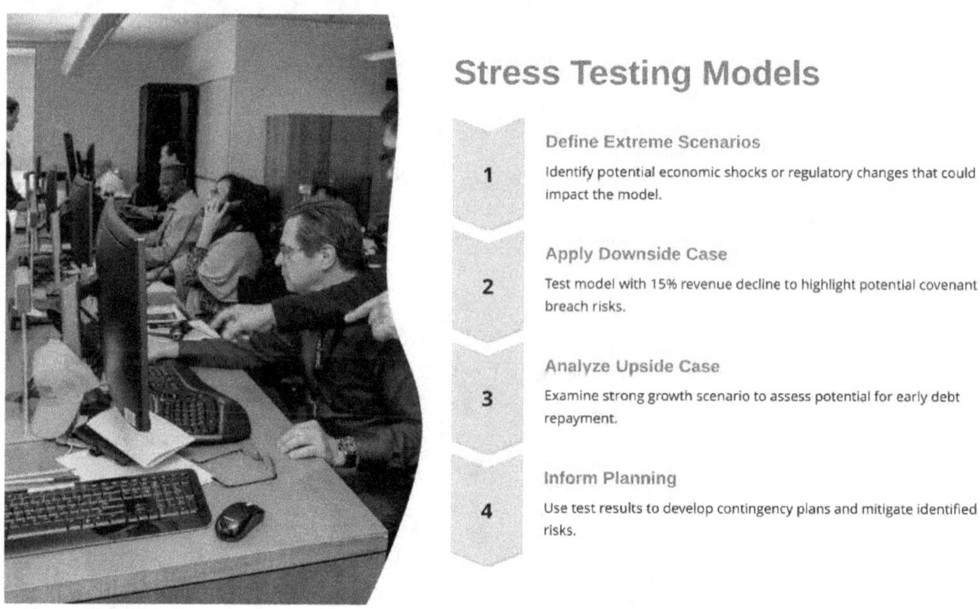

4.3 Real-Time Adjustments

Modern data analytics tools and cloud-based modeling platforms enable sponsors to **update valuations in real time**:

1. **Market Dynamics**
    - If interest rates climb unexpectedly, sponsors can quickly adjust the model to see how higher borrowing costs affect IRR and debt coverage.
    - Changes in comparable company multiples or macroeconomic indicators can also prompt real-time revaluations.
2. **Operational Metrics**
    - IoT sensors or advanced inventory-tracking systems can give near-instant feedback on production yields, sales volumes, or supply chain bottlenecks.
    - This data can feed into rolling forecasts for more accurate monthly or quarterly updates.

Self-Study Questions

1. **Define Enterprise Value (EV)** and explain why it's a preferred metric for LBO sponsors over simple market capitalization.
2. **Discuss how sensitivity analysis** can uncover vulnerabilities in an LBO model. Which specific variables (e.g., revenue growth, EBITDA margin) have the greatest impact in most scenarios?
3. **Outline the five key steps** in building an LBO model, highlighting why each step is critical for decision-making.
4. **What role do ESG metrics play** in modern LBO valuations? Illustrate how ESG-related factors might shift both risk and return expectations.
5. **Create a sensitivity table** showing IRR variations based on two variables (for example, revenue growth and EBITDA margin). Which combination yields the highest IRR, and why?

Sources and Uses

The sources and uses below outlines transaction financing and fund allocation.

Sources

- Debt contributions
- Equity contributions

Uses

- Purchase price
- Transaction fees
- Working capital needs

These sources and uses ensure transparency and aligns stakeholders, showing how every dollar is utilized.

Lesson Takeaways

1. **Core Valuation Methods**: EV, EBITDA multiples, and DCF form the bedrock of LBO valuation, each offering different perspectives on value and risk.
2. **Proactive Risk Assessment**: Sensitivity and scenario analyses reveal how fragile or robust an LBO's returns are under varying market conditions.
3. **Robust LBO Models**: A well-constructed financial model encompasses input assumptions, sources/uses of funds, multi-year projections, debt schedules, and robust return metrics (IRR, cash-on-cash).
4. **ESG & Advanced Techniques**: Modern LBOs increasingly incorporate ESG considerations and real-time data to capture intangible benefits and risks, refine valuations, and support ongoing decision-making post-acquisition.
5. **Adaptability**: Integrating stress testing and dynamic updates ensures the LBO model can adjust to real-world changes—economic, regulatory, or operational—enhancing the investment's odds of long-term success.

Financial Projections and Debt Schedules

Comprehensive Forecasts

LBO models require 5-10 year projections for income statement, balance sheet, and cash flow.

Operational Insights

Projections incorporate operational shifts and net working capital changes for forward-looking perspective.

Debt Management

Debt schedules track repayment profiles, interest expenses, and potential refinancing opportunities.

Cash Flow Focus

Emphasis on cash flow reliance in debt schedules and financial projections.

References and Further Reading

1. **Damodaran, A. (2012).** *Investment Valuation: Tools and Techniques for Determining the Value of Any Asset.* Wiley.
2. **Rosenbaum, J., & Pearl, J. (2020).** *Investment Banking: Valuation, Leveraged Buyouts, and Mergers & Acquisitions.* Wiley.
3. **Kaplan, S. N., & Strömberg, P. (2009).** *Leveraged Buyouts and Private Equity. Journal of Economic Perspectives.*
4. Case Studies on **Advanced LBO Modeling** from VCII Institute.
5. **Private Equity Insights**: Articles on ESG integration and real-time data analytics in LBO transactions.

Lesson 4: Strategic Execution

Lesson Objectives

By the end of this lesson, participants will be able to:

1. **Master pre-acquisition analysis techniques** for identifying and securing high-potential LBO targets.
2. **Design and implement post-acquisition strategies** that maximize value creation and operational improvements.
3. **Develop robust frameworks** for aligning management incentives with sponsor objectives.
4. **Understand and apply advanced monitoring and performance tracking systems** for portfolio companies.

Deal Sourcing and Screening Process

1. **Network Leverage**
   Sponsors tap into their existing networks, including industry contacts and financial advisors, to identify potential targets.
2. **Intermediary Relationships**
   Investment banks, brokers, and other intermediaries play a vital role in deal flow by connecting sponsors with companies.
3. **Data Analytics**
   Sophisticated data analytics tools allow sponsors to sift through vast amounts of information and identify companies with promising characteristics.

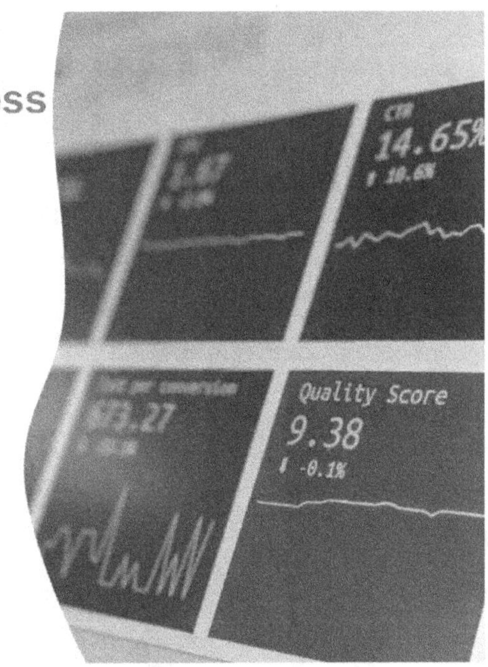

Lesson Content

1. Pre-Acquisition Analysis

Strategic execution for an LBO begins **long before** the ink dries on the purchase agreement. A meticulously planned pre-acquisition phase allows sponsors to **identify the right targets**, **mitigate deal risks**, and **secure favorable terms**. This phase spans deal sourcing, rigorous due diligence, and artful negotiation, creating a foundation for future post-acquisition success.

1.1 Deal Sourcing and Screening

1. Proactive Deal Sourcing

- **Leveraging Networks**: Private equity (PE) sponsors, investment groups, and corporate buyers tap into deep networks of industry experts, bankers, brokers, and even target-company executives to uncover deals.
- **Intermediaries**: Investment banks, brokers, and management teams often broker introductions, but **proprietary deals** sourced directly through relationships can yield lower acquisition multiples and reduced competition.
- **Regional and Sector Focus**: Some sponsors maintain specialized sector knowledge—like industrial technology or renewable energy—and keep close tabs on emerging trends, making them better positioned to uncover hidden gems.

2. Screening Criteria

- **Financial Metrics**: Assess EBITDA size, free cash flow stability, and existing leverage. Many PE firms have **hard floors** for minimum EBITDA (e.g., $10M or $50M) to ensure scale and profitability.
- **Market Position**: Scrutinize competitive advantage, defensibility of market share, and barriers to entry. Targets with strong brand equity or patented technology often command premium valuations but also bring robust upside potential.
- **Operational Opportunities**: Look for a **clear "value-add"** angle, whether through cost streamlining, revenue expansion, or strategic refocus.

Negotiating Purchase Agreements

Price

A fair price balances the target's value with the acquirer's budget.

Terms

Payment structure and closing timeline are critical for both sides.

Protections

Earn-outs ensure deal success by aligning incentives.

Advanced Techniques in Deal Sourcing

- **Data Analytics and AI**: Platforms like PitchBook, PrivCo, and other proprietary databases can feed machine-learning models that flag companies meeting specific metrics—revenue growth rates, margin profiles, or niche market segments.
- **Industry-Focused Networks**: Participation in specialized industry conferences or trade associations can uncover sector-specific targets that broader searches miss.
- **Co-Investment Partnerships**: Collaborating with regional private equity firms or strategic corporate partners can offer localized insights and reduce blind spots in unfamiliar geographies.

1.2 Due Diligence

Due diligence is the process of validating assumptions, unearthing hidden pitfalls, and refining the deal's valuation prior to signing. Sponsors often engage **multidisciplinary teams** of experts—accountants, lawyers, operational specialists—to minimize surprises post-close.

1. Financial Due Diligence

- **Historical Performance**: Deep-dive into the target's revenue trends, EBITDA margins, and free cash flow generation. Historical data can reveal cyclical patterns or one-off events that inflate (or deflate) earnings.
- **Debt Sustainability**: Assess existing leverage and forecast whether future operating cash flows can comfortably service new LBO debt.
- **Projection Validation**: Management's growth forecasts might be optimistic. Sponsors often source independent industry data to test these assumptions.

2. Operational Due Diligence

- **Efficiency Assessments**: Analyze manufacturing processes, distribution networks, and supply chain logistics. Even modest process improvements—like automating a production line—can significantly boost EBITDA.
- **Technology Integration**: Evaluate IT infrastructure, cybersecurity readiness, and scalability of software systems. High-growth companies require robust tech stacks to handle expansion.
- **Human Capital Analysis**: Identify key employees, skill gaps, and cultural strengths/weaknesses. Strong management teams can expedite value creation post-close.

3. Legal and Regulatory Due Diligence

- **Compliance Audits**: Confirm adherence to labor laws, environmental regulations, and sector-specific rules. Fines and legal penalties can derail returns if uncovered post-acquisition.
- **Contract Reviews**: Evaluate major customer, supplier, or partnership agreements to identify any **change-of-control** or termination clauses triggered by the LBO.
- **Intellectual Property**: Verify ownership of patents, trademarks, or trade secrets. In technology or biotech deals, IP can represent a major share of enterprise value.

4. Market Due Diligence

- **Industry Trends**: Map out macroeconomic shifts, customer behavior, and competitor strategies. A target in a declining segment may not be worth a high multiple unless there's a clear turnaround plan.

- **Risk Assessments**: Factor in potential disruptors—e.g., new regulations, technological upheavals, or geopolitical shifts.
- **Geographic Considerations**: If the company operates in multiple regions, sponsors should evaluate each region's growth prospects, regulatory hurdles, and cultural nuances.

Due Diligence

1. **Risk Assessment**
   Due diligence uncovers potential risks and challenges that could impact the investment.
2. **Financial Validation**
   Teams verify the accuracy of financial statements and assess the target's overall financial health.
3. **Market Analysis**
   The team examines market trends, competitive landscape, and potential growth opportunities for the target.

Exhibit 1: Key Areas of Due Diligence

- **Financial**: Revenue, EBITDA, cash flow stability
- **Operational**: Cost structure, supply chain, production efficiency
- **Legal and Regulatory**: Compliance, IP ownership, pending litigation
- **Market**: Industry outlook, competitive landscape, potential disruptors

1.3 Negotiating Purchase Agreements and Terms

After due diligence clarifies the target's value and risk profile, the sponsor negotiates a **purchase agreement** outlining the acquisition price, representations, warranties, and covenants.

1. **Valuation and Pricing**
   - Sponsors typically anchor on **EBITDA multiples**, DCF analyses, or a blend of these.
   - Insights from due diligence can highlight operational shortfalls—justifying a lower multiple—or prove unexploited growth vectors that may support a higher price.
2. **Representations and Warranties**
   - Legal clauses ensure sellers disclose all liabilities or potential issues. If undisclosed problems surface post-deal, sponsors can seek remedies or price adjustments.
3. **Earn-Out Clauses**
   - A portion of the purchase price might hinge on future performance, bridging valuation gaps and sharing upside (or downside) between buyer and seller.
4. **Covenants**
   - Define what the seller must or must not do prior to closing (e.g., taking on new debt, signing long-term contracts).
   - Prevents material changes that could degrade the target's value.

Advanced Negotiation Techniques

- **Contingent Value Rights (CVRs)**: Link additional payments to milestones (product approvals in pharma, hitting revenue targets in consumer goods).
- **Adjustable Covenants**: Some covenants shift in response to external indices (e.g., interest rates, commodity prices), giving both parties flexibility in volatile markets.

2. Post-Acquisition Strategy

Once the deal closes, the spotlight shifts to **executing** on operational, strategic, and financial improvements that **translate** purchase assumptions into **real-world returns**.

2.1 Operational Improvements and Value Creation Initiatives

Sponsors pursue a range of tactics to enhance EBITDA, tighten cost structures, and unlock revenue growth:

1. Cost Optimization

- **Streamlining Operations**: Centralize procurement across business units, standardize IT systems, or consolidate redundant facilities to cut overhead.
- **Negotiating Vendor Contracts**: Harness the sponsor's broader relationships to secure volume discounts or preferential supply deals.
- **Automation and AI**: Deploy robotics in manufacturing or RPA (Robotic Process Automation) in administrative workflows to reduce labor intensity.

2. Revenue Growth

- **Market Share Expansion**: Bolster digital marketing, refine product positioning, or add distribution channels (e.g., e-commerce for traditional brick-and-mortar brands).
- **Product Diversification**: Develop adjacent product lines that leverage existing brand equity or cross-sell to a loyal customer base.
- **Geographic Expansion**: Tap into fast-growing international markets, often by leveraging local partnerships to navigate regulatory or cultural nuances.

3. Strategic Realignment

- **Core Focus**: If the company is juggling multiple divisions, sponsors may divest non-core segments and allocate capital where ROIC (return on invested capital) is highest.
- **Bolt-On Acquisitions**: Acquire smaller complementary firms to expand capabilities or enter new market niches. This approach can accelerate growth while capturing synergies.

Exhibit 2: Value Creation Initiatives

- **Cost Optimization**: Centralized procurement, overhead reduction
- **Revenue Growth**: E-commerce expansion, loyalty programs, new product lines
- **Strategic Realignment**: Divesting non-core assets, pursuing bolt-on deals

2.2 Monitoring Performance

Ongoing performance management is critical to ensure the portfolio company stays on track:

1. **Key Performance Indicators (KPIs)**
   - **Financial KPIs**: EBITDA margin, free cash flow, debt reduction rate.
   - **Operational KPIs**: Production lead times, customer churn, inventory turnover.
   - **Strategic KPIs**: Market share, new product launches, M&A pipeline.
2. **Board Oversight**
   - Sponsors typically establish a **board of directors** that includes sponsor representatives, industry experts, and company executives. Regular board meetings address performance variances and strategic pivots.
   - Independent directors can provide external perspectives and challenge assumptions, fostering transparency.
3. **Interim Adjustments**
   - Sponsors continuously assess whether the initial plan remains viable in shifting market conditions—e.g., economic downturns, competitor moves, or technological disruptions.
   - Quick pivots might involve reallocating budget from underperforming divisions to more promising lines of business or accelerating a digital transformation plan.

2.3 Aligning Management Incentives

A key differentiator in successful LBOs is how well the sponsor's goals align with those of the **management team**:

1. **Equity Participation**
   - Management often receives a **carried interest** or equity stake—tying personal wealth creation to the firm's long-term success.
   - Vesting schedules (3–5 years) foster retention and continuity.
2. **Performance-Based Bonuses**
   - Bonuses tied to revenue or EBITDA milestones spur short-term execution while preserving the big picture.
   - Some LBOs feature "ratchet mechanisms" that offer **escalating equity stakes** if managers exceed certain return thresholds.
3. **Clear Communication**
   - Sponsors should articulate the strategic vision, set realistic targets, and encourage a culture of accountability.
   - Regular check-ins (monthly or quarterly) keep management motivated, highlight successes, and address emerging issues proactively.

Exhibit 3: Incentive Mechanisms

- **Equity Participation**: Management holds 5–15% equity stake
- **Performance Bonuses**: Tied to EBITDA or revenue milestones
- **Vesting Schedules**: Equity awards vest over 3–5 years

3. Case Study: The Post-Acquisition Journey of "RetailCo"

Background

- RetailCo, a mid-sized retail chain, was acquired via an LBO for $800 million.
- The deal consisted of $500 million in debt and $300 million in sponsor equity.

Challenges

- High operating costs due to scattered distribution centers and aging inventory systems.
- Declining same-store sales driven by a shift in consumer behavior toward online shopping.

Post-Acquisition Strategy

1. **Cost Optimization**:
    - Consolidated five distribution centers into two strategically located hubs, cutting logistics expenses by 15%.
    - Automated repetitive inventory tasks, reducing labor requirements.
2. **Revenue Growth**:
    - Launched a user-friendly e-commerce platform, which accounted for 20% of total revenue within two years.
    - Expanded into suburban regions with favorable demographics, adding 30 new stores near high-traffic shopping plazas.
3. **Strategic Realignment**:
    - Divested underperforming apparel lines, reinvesting proceeds into higher-margin home goods.
    - Entered a bolt-on acquisition of a local furniture retailer, creating cross-selling opportunities that boosted average ticket size.

Results

- **EBITDA** rose from $80 million to $140 million in three years.
- The sponsor's **IRR** reached 25%, surpassing the initial target of 18%.
- Management, holding a 10% equity stake, realized substantial personal gains, fueling further collaboration and trust.

Self-Study Questions

1. **What are the key components** of pre-acquisition analysis in an LBO, and why are they vital to choosing the right target?
2. **How can operational improvements** drive post-acquisition value creation? Provide examples of both cost optimization and revenue growth tactics.
3. **Discuss the role of KPIs** in monitoring the performance of portfolio companies. Which financial and operational KPIs might be most critical?
4. **Explain the importance** of aligning management incentives with sponsor objectives. What mechanisms can sponsors deploy to ensure alignment?
5. **Using a hypothetical company**, outline a post-acquisition strategy focusing on cost optimization, revenue growth, and strategic realignment.

Implementing Post-Acquisition Strategies

Lesson Takeaways

- **Effective Pre-Acquisition Analysis**: Thorough deal sourcing, screening, and due diligence set the stage for finding the right target and mitigating risks before the deal closes.
- **Operational and Strategic Levers**: Sponsors unlock value through cost efficiency, revenue expansion, and strategic realignments that capitalize on the target's strengths.
- **Monitoring and Accountability**: A structured system of KPIs, board oversight, and agile adaptations ensures the portfolio company remains on track to achieve (or exceed) underwritten returns.
- **Management Alignment**: Equity participation and performance-based incentives are vital tools to motivate leadership and foster a unified vision.
- **Case Studies**: Real-world examples, like RetailCo, demonstrate how strategic execution can revitalize a stagnant company, achieve significant EBITDA growth, and deliver robust returns.

Aligning Management Incentives

Equity Stakes

Managers with equity stakes are incentivized to increase company value, aligning their interests with investors.

Performance Bonuses

Performance-based bonuses reward managers for exceeding targets, driving accountability and high performance.

Clear Communication

Transparent communication about goals and performance metrics ensures alignment and fosters a sense of shared purpose.

References and Further Reading

1. **Gilligan, J., & Wright, M. (2020).** *Private Equity Demystified: An Explanatory Guide.* Oxford University Press.

2. **Teten, D., & Farmer, C. (2021).** *How Private Equity Firms Hire CEOs for Their Portfolio Companies.* Journal of Investment Management.

3. **Baker, G. P., & Montgomery, C. A. (2009).** *Performance Pressure and the Investment Strategies of Private Equity Firms.* Harvard Business Review.

4. **Bain & Company. (2022).** *Global Private Equity Report.*

5. **McKinsey & Company. (2021).** *Creating Value Through Portfolio Companies: A Guide for PE Sponsors.*

Lesson 5: Practical Case Studies and Real-World Applications

Lesson Objectives

By the end of this lesson, participants will be able to:

1. **Analyze iconic LBO transactions** across different regions and industries.
2. **Understand strategies** employed in successful LBOs and the factors that contributed to their outcomes.
3. **Learn from failed LBOs**, identifying common pitfalls and ways to mitigate risks.
4. **Apply insights** from real-world case studies to future LBO opportunities.

Lesson Content

1. Global Insights: Iconic LBOs Across Regions

Over the past several decades, **leveraged buyouts** have become a global phenomenon, with each region offering unique **regulatory environments, cultural nuances, and market dynamics**. Examining LBOs in the United States, Europe, and the Middle East/North Africa (MENA) region reveals how strategies can vary widely—and how certain universal principles still apply.

1.1 United States: The Birthplace of Modern LBOs

The U.S. has a long history of high-profile LBOs, often featuring aggressive financial engineering and sophisticated deal structures.

Case 1: RJR Nabisco (1988)

- **Deal Overview**: A $25 billion buyout by Kohlberg Kravis Roberts (KKR), widely seen as a defining moment in the "LBO boom" of the 1980s. Chronicled in the book *Barbarians at the Gate*, this transaction remains a landmark for its scale and controversy.
- **Key Strategies**
  1. **Aggressive Financial Engineering**: Heavy use of high-yield ("junk") bonds underpinned the colossal leverage, pushing the limits of what credit markets would tolerate.
  2. **Leveraged Financing and Bidding War**: Multiple bidders, including management, drove up the purchase price. KKR ultimately won with an offer loaded with leverage.
- **Lessons Learned**
  1. **Transformative Power of Financial Structuring**: Even well-established conglomerates could be taken private if credit markets were receptive.
  2. **Risks of Over-Leverage**: High debt service requirements and market volatility sparked discussions about the sustainability of such deals and led to increased regulatory scrutiny.

Case 2: Hilton Hotels (2007)

- **Deal Overview**: Blackstone Group acquired Hilton Hotels for $26 billion, in what became one of the largest hospitality LBOs of its era.
- **Key Strategies**

1. **Operational Improvements**: Centralizing management of global properties and implementing standardized best practices across the chain.
2. **Digital Transformation & Asset-Light Model**: Enhancing online booking systems and refocusing on franchised or managed properties rather than owning real estate.

- **Lessons Learned**

1. **Operational Efficiency + Expansion**: Showed how a global brand could leverage scale and technology to improve margins and market share.
2. **Resilience Through Strategic Focus**: Emphasized that combining real estate and hospitality expertise can drive strong post-acquisition returns, even in a cyclical industry.

Deal Name	Key Strategies	Lessons Learned
RJR Nabisco	High-yield bonds, aggressive leveraging	Risks of over-leverage; regulatory scrutiny
Hilton Hotels	Operational efficiency, digital expansion	Strategic alignment with global growth opportunities

1.2 Europe: Focus on Operational Turnaround

In Europe, LBOs often revolve around **operational improvements** and consolidations, partly due to the region's more stringent labor laws, complex cross-border regulations, and mature industries.

Case 3: Boots Alliance (2007)

- **Deal Overview**: Alliance Boots was acquired by KKR and Stefano Pessina for £11 billion, marking Europe's first pharmacy-led LBO of this magnitude.
- **Key Strategies**
    1. **Supply Chain Streamlining**: Standardized procurement, optimized warehousing, and centralized logistics to cut costs.
    2. **Retail Consolidation**: Focused on high-margin product categories (beauty, health products) and leveraged the Boots brand recognition.
- **Lessons Learned**
    1. **Power of Operational Efficiency**: Demonstrated that even in **mature markets**, targeted process improvements can significantly boost EBITDA.
    2. **Supply Chain Optimization**: Vital to achieving cost savings in large-scale retail or pharmacy chains.

Case 4: Altice and SFR (2014)

- **Deal Overview**: Patrick Drahi's Altice acquired SFR, a French telecom operator, in a $17 billion transaction.
- **Key Strategies**
    1. **Aggressive Cost-Cutting**: Rationalized overhead, reduced headcount, and renegotiated supplier contracts.
    2. **Bundled Services**: Combined internet, phone, and cable services to improve customer retention and ARPU (average revenue per user).
- **Lessons Learned**
    1. **High Leverage in Capital-Intensive Sectors**: Telecom deals can be lucrative but leave little margin for error if revenue growth slows or CAPEX requirements spike.
    2. **Importance of Customer Stickiness**: Bundled offerings can stabilize cash flows but require careful management of quality and service differentiation.

Region	Deal Name	Key Strategy	Industry Insights
Europe	Boots Alliance	Supply chain and retail consolidation	Operational efficiencies in mature markets
Europe	Altice and SFR	Cost-cutting, bundled services	Critical to maintain customer loyalty in capital-intensive telecom

1.3 Middle East and North Africa (MENA): Family Businesses and Privatization

Many MENA LBOs revolve around **family-owned conglomerates** or state-led privatization efforts, posing unique cultural, regulatory, and geopolitical considerations.

Case 5: Kuwait Food Company (Americana) (2016)

- **Deal Overview**: UAE-based Adeptio acquired a majority stake in Kuwait's Americana for $2.4 billion, taking control of well-known franchises like KFC and Pizza Hut in the region.
- **Key Strategies**
  1. **Restructuring Family-Owned Operations**: Introducing more corporate governance and professional management to drive efficiency.
  2. **Leveraging Regional Consumer Preferences**: Expanding product lines that cater to local tastes while optimizing marketing across multiple Gulf Cooperation Council (GCC) countries.
- **Lessons Learned**
  1. **Cultural Considerations**: Transitioning a decades-old family enterprise to a more standardized operational model requires careful stakeholder management.
  2. **Tailoring Strategy to Regional Demographics**: A younger, rapidly growing population in the GCC can amplify returns if expansions are well-executed.

Case 6: Banque du Caire (Privatization Effort)

- **Deal Overview**: A state-led initiative to privatize one of Egypt's major banks via an LBO-like structure, with international PE firms involved in management.
- **Key Strategies**
  1. **PE Expertise in a Legacy Institution**: Streamlining outdated processes and introducing advanced digital banking solutions.
  2. **Technological Modernization**: Upgrading core banking systems to improve service delivery and compete with private-sector banks.
- **Lessons Learned**
  1. **Potential of Privatization + PE**: Merging state-owned assets with private equity know-how can unlock latent value.

2. **Digital Transformation**: Legacy banking sectors are ripe for technology overhauls, which can differentiate a newly privatized entity.

Case Study: Americana

Adeptio's Acquisition

Restructured family-owned business into streamlined corporate entity

Key Strategies

Professionalized management, expanded offerings for local tastes

Success Factors

Cultural adaptation, regional market insights

The Americana case study highlights the importance of understanding local markets in LBO success. By adapting to regional preferences and modernizing operations, Adeptio transformed a legacy business into a competitive corporate entity.

2. Industry-Specific Strategies: Case Studies by Sector

Beyond regional variations, LBOs also differ by **industry characteristics**, such as regulatory intensity, capital requirements, and rate of technological disruption. This section explores key sector-focused LBOs, highlighting how unique factors shape deal success.

2.1 Healthcare: HCA Healthcare (2006)

- **Deal Overview**: Acquired by Bain Capital, KKR, and Merrill Lynch for $33 billion, making it one of the largest healthcare buyouts at the time.
- **Key Strategies**
    1. **Operational Optimization**: Standardizing hospital operations and reducing administrative overhead to improve margins.
    2. **Investment in Technology**: Implementing electronic health records (EHR) and other IT solutions to streamline patient care, billing, and compliance.
- **Insights**
    1. **Regulatory Complexity**: Healthcare deals require navigating ever-changing regulations and reimbursement models, demanding specialized knowledge.
    2. **Scalability**: Once a robust operational framework was established, additional hospitals or clinics could be integrated more seamlessly.

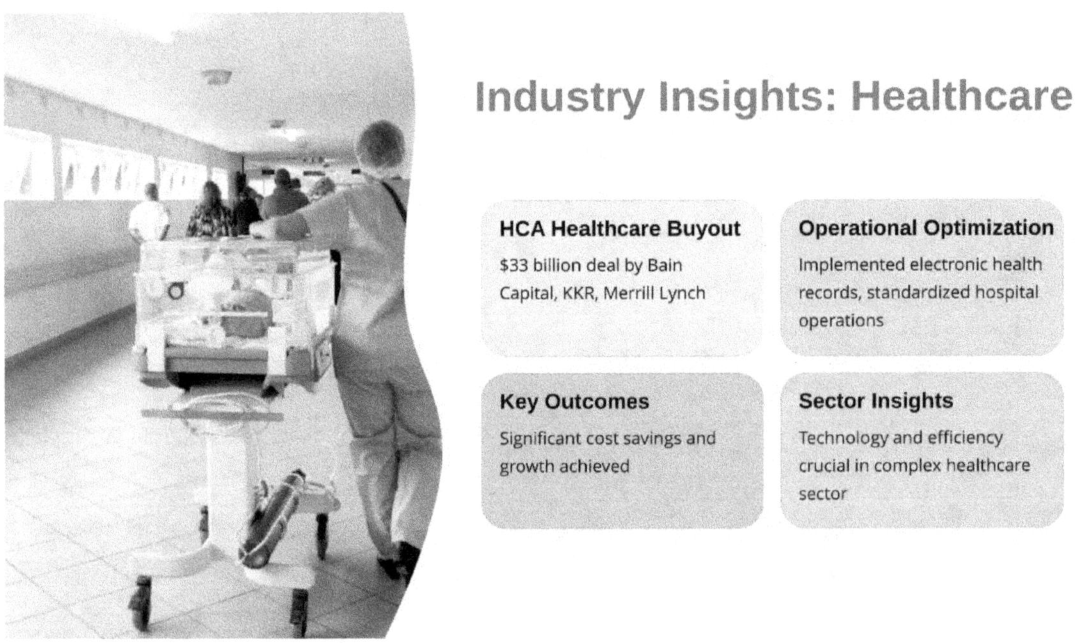

2.2 Technology: Dell (2013)

- **Deal Overview**: Michael Dell partnered with Silver Lake Partners to take Dell private in a $24.9 billion transaction, aiming to pivot from a PC-based model to enterprise solutions.
- **Key Strategies**
    1. **Refocusing on Cloud and Enterprise**: Diverting resources from low-margin hardware to higher-margin data center and software offerings.
    2. **R&D Investments**: Allocating significant capital to innovation, including server technology, storage solutions, and cybersecurity.
- **Insights**
    1. **Founder-Led Strategic Vision**: Michael Dell's leadership and deep familiarity with the company allowed decisive shifts in product strategy.
    2. **Long-Term Value**: Taking the company private reduced quarterly earnings pressure, facilitating more transformative changes over multiple years.

2.3 Manufacturing: Chrysler (2007)

- **Deal Overview**: Cerberus Capital Management acquired an 80.1% stake in Chrysler for $7.4 billion from Daimler.
- **Key Strategies**
    1. **Production Realignment**: Streamlining factories, eliminating unprofitable models, and focusing on trucks and SUVs.
    2. **Brand Revitalization**: Attempting to revamp designs and marketing to compete with foreign automakers.
- **Insights**
    1. **Legacy Challenges**: Union labor contracts, pension obligations, and high fixed costs made turnaround efforts more complex.
    2. **Market Saturation**: The U.S. automotive market was intensely competitive, leaving little room for missteps.

Sector	Case Study	Key Insight	Strategy
Healthcare	HCA Healthcare	Operational optimization saves costs	Invest in technology to streamline care & billing
Technology	Dell	Pivot to cloud computing & enterprise focus	R&D investments, long-term product realignment
Manufacturing	Chrysler	Challenges in legacy car manufacturing	Cost reductions, brand overhaul, union negotiations

3. Lessons from Failures: Common Pitfalls and Mitigation Strategies

While many LBOs generate impressive returns, others fall short—often due to **excessive leverage**, **unrealistic growth assumptions**, or **inadequate operational execution**. Examining failed deals highlights the pitfalls that sponsors must avoid.

3.1 Missteps in Capital Structuring

Case 7: TXU Energy (2007)

- **Deal Overview**: A $45 billion buyout led by KKR and TPG Capital, aiming to capitalize on stable energy demand and expected deregulation benefits.
- **What Went Wrong**
  1. **Excessive Leverage**: The deal heavily relied on debt, leaving no cushion when natural gas prices fell and environmental regulations tightened.
  2. **Regulatory Changes**: Emerging concerns over carbon emissions and stricter policies on coal plants undercut TXU's core business model.
- **Lessons Learned**
  1. **Anticipate External Shocks**: Sponsors must stress-test assumptions, especially in industries vulnerable to commodity price swings or policy shifts.
  2. **Avoid Over-Reliance on Debt**: A balanced capital structure with manageable debt load is crucial for navigating economic headwinds.

Fictional Case: Retail Chain XYZ

- **What Went Wrong**
  1. **Aggressive Repayment Timelines**: High interest rates and short maturities led to liquidity crises.
  2. **Insufficient Free Cash Flow**: Operational margins couldn't support mandated debt payments, forcing asset sales at unfavorable valuations.
- **Lessons Learned**
  1. **Realistic Debt-to-Equity Ratios**: Sponsors must align leverage with stable cash flow expectations.
  2. **Flexibility in Financing**: Longer maturities or mezzanine layers can offer breathing room.

3.2 Operational Management Failures

Case 8: Toys "R" Us (2017)

- **Deal Overview**: Bain Capital, KKR, and Vornado Realty Trust acquired Toys "R" Us for $6.6 billion in 2005, but the company declared bankruptcy in 2017.
- **What Went Wrong**
    1. **Ignoring E-commerce Trends**: Failing to adapt to online competition (Amazon, Walmart) eroded market share.
    2. **High Debt Costs**: Servicing debt drained resources that could have funded digital investments, store renovations, or improved supply chains.
- **Lessons Learned**
    1. **Align Strategy with Market Evolution**: In retail, especially, ignoring shifting consumer behaviors is lethal.
    2. **Preserve CapEx for Innovation**: Over-leveraging can starve a company's ability to invest in strategic pivots.

Case Study: Toys "R" Us

Over-leveraging

Drained resources needed for innovation and growth

E-commerce neglect

Failed to adapt to online shopping trends

Market share loss

Competitors overtook due to strategic missteps

Toys "R" Us failure emphasizes importance of aligning strategies with consumer behavior and preserving capital for growth.

Fictional Case: "TechCo"

- **What Went Wrong**

  1. **Poor Integration of Acquired Assets**: Multiple bolt-on acquisitions remained siloed, causing duplication of effort and inconsistent product lines.
  2. **Mismanagement of Human Capital**: High turnover and a lack of cultural alignment hampered collaboration.

- **Lessons Learned**

  1. **Integration Planning**: Sponsors need thorough post-acquisition frameworks to merge teams, systems, and processes.
  2. **Talent Retention**: Equity incentives, clear career paths, and cultural coherence are key to sustaining momentum.

Failure Area	Case Study	Lessons Learned
Capital Structuring	TXU Energy	Anticipate market/regulatory risks, avoid over-leverage
Operational Management	Toys "R" Us	Adapt strategies to market changes, preserve innovation budgets

Self-Study Questions

1. **Compare and contrast** the strategies employed in the Hilton Hotels and Boots Alliance LBOs. How did operational focus shape their outcomes?

2. **What are the key takeaways** from the failure of TXU Energy, and how can practitioners mitigate similar risks in future LBOs?

3. **Analyze the role of technology** in the success of the Dell LBO. How can strategic tech investments drive value creation, especially in legacy businesses?

4. **Identify and discuss** the unique challenges faced in MENA-region LBOs, such as the Kuwait Food Company acquisition. How do cultural, regulatory, or family business factors come into play?

5. **Based on the Toys "R" Us failure**, propose a framework for integrating market trends (like e-commerce) into operational strategy early in the post-acquisition phase.

Lesson Takeaways

- **Regional Nuances**: Iconic LBOs around the world—from the U.S. and Europe to MENA—demonstrate that local regulations, cultural factors, and market structures heavily influence deal strategy.
- **Sector-Specific Approaches**: Healthcare, tech, and manufacturing each present distinct challenges (regulatory hurdles, high capital requirements, rapid innovation cycles) that require targeted solutions.
- **Failures as Learning Tools**: High-profile collapses like TXU Energy and Toys "R" Us underscore the perils of excessive leverage, ignoring technological shifts, and mismanaging post-acquisition integration.
- **Agile and Forward-Looking**: Successful LBOs adapt operations, harness data and technology, and keep an ear to evolving consumer trends. Maintaining a balanced capital structure offers a buffer against external shocks.
- **Practitioner Mindset**: Continual refinement based on real-world case studies is critical. Sponsors, advisors, and management teams should remain vigilant about shifting market conditions, regulatory changes, and operational demands.

References and Further Reading

1. **Teten, D., & Farmer, C. (2021).** *Case Studies in Private Equity Execution.* Journal of Investment Strategies.
2. **Bain & Company. (2022).** *LBO Lessons: Global Trends and Best Practices.*
3. **McKinsey & Company. (2021).** *Operational Excellence in Leveraged Buyouts.*
4. **Harvard Business School Case Studies. (2020).** *Iconic LBO Deals: Success and Failure.*
5. **Gilligan, J., & Wright, M. (2020).** *Global Perspectives on Private Equity and Buyouts.* Oxford University Press.

Lesson 6: LBO Excel and Modeling Primer

Lesson Objectives

By the end of this lesson, participants will be able to:

1. **Understand the essential structure and components** of a leveraged buyout (LBO) model in Excel.
2. **Master core Excel tools and functions** that streamline the financial modeling process.
3. **Utilize advanced techniques**—including scenario analysis, macros, and robust error checking—to create dynamic models.
4. **Avoid common pitfalls** by adhering to best practices in accuracy, usability, and version control.

Why Excel for LBOs?

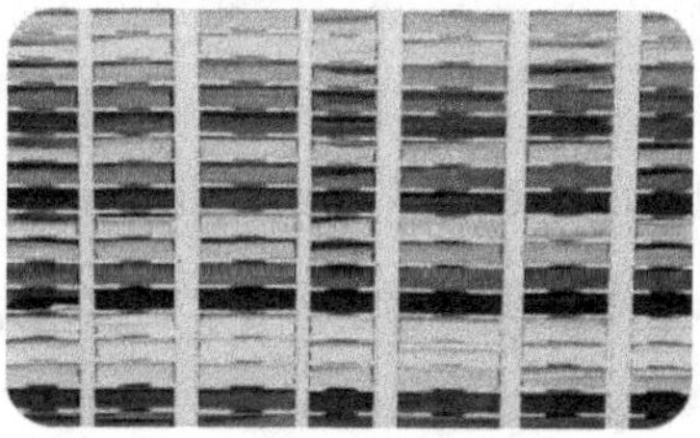

Versatility

Excel's grid structure enables logical organization and real-time adjustments.

Industry Standard

Excel dominates finance due to its accessibility and adaptability.

Scenario Analysis

Excel allows for easy creation and comparison of different LBO scenarios.

Excel remains the preferred tool for LBO modeling across industries, despite dedicated software alternatives.

Lesson Content

1. Overview of Excel for LBO Modeling

Why Excel?
Despite the emergence of dedicated modeling software, Excel remains the **standard** in the finance industry due to its **flexibility**, **accessibility**, and **compatibility** with vast data sets. An LBO model built in Excel offers customizable frameworks, real-time scenario testing, and intuitive presentation capabilities for stakeholders.

1.1 Key Requirements for an Effective LBO Model

1. **Logical Structure and Organization**
    - **Clear Tab Segmentation**: Separate the workbook into logical sections:
        - **Assumptions** (inputs)
        - **Financial Statements** (income statement, balance sheet, cash flow)
        - **Debt Schedule** (amortization, interest, covenants)
        - **Output/Summary** (IRR, DSCR, charts, key metrics)
    - **Uniform Formatting**: Assign consistent color schemes for inputs, calculations, and references (e.g., **blue** for inputs, **black** for calculations, **green** for external links). This color-coding system accelerates comprehension and error-tracking.
    - **Cell Labeling**: Use descriptive row and column labels so that each number can be quickly identified by the user or reviewer.
2. **Accuracy and Efficiency**
    - **Validation Tools**: Implement data validation (e.g., drop-down lists for scenario toggles) and conditional formatting to catch anomalies (like negative EBITDA).
    - **Keyboard Shortcuts**: Embrace shortcuts for everyday tasks (e.g., **Ctrl + Shift + L** for filters, **Alt + E + S + V** for "paste special → values"), drastically reducing keystrokes.
    - **Version Control**: Keep a change log or use file naming conventions with timestamps (e.g., "LBO_Model_v1_2025-01-05.xlsx") so you can revert if an error creeps in.
3. **Flexibility for Scenario Analysis**
    - **Dynamic Inputs**: Hard-code as little as possible; reference all major assumptions (growth rates, exit multiples, interest rates) from the Assumptions tab.

- **Responsive Dashboards**: Create summary tables and charts that instantly reflect new data when you alter key variables.

Pro Tip: Overly complex models can hamper clarity. Focus on the **key value drivers**—leverage, cash flow generation, revenue growth, exit assumptions—rather than crowding the model with immaterial details.

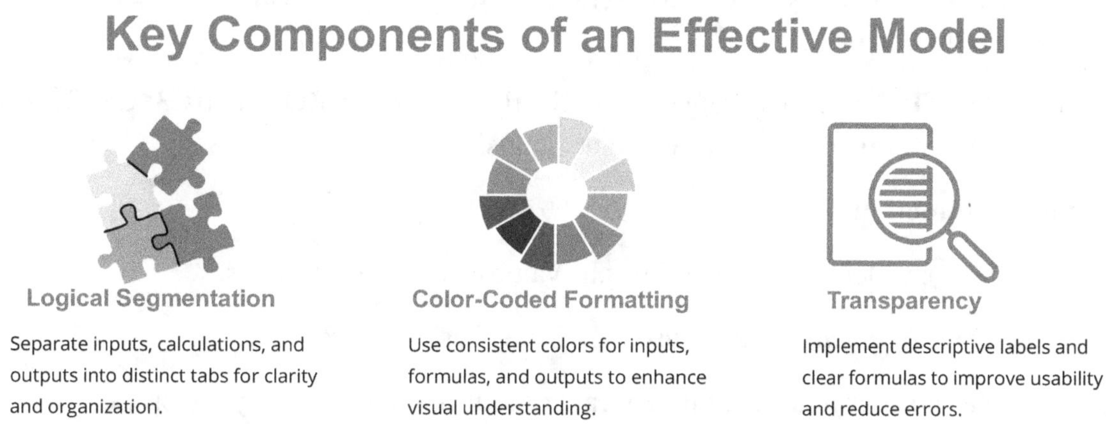

2. Essential Excel Tools for LBO Modeling

Excel's built-in functions and features can handle a wide range of tasks essential to LBO analysis: from basic arithmetic to discount rates and internal rate of return (IRR) calculations.

2.1 Core Functions and Formulas

1. **Mathematical Functions**
    - **SUM(), AVERAGE(), MIN(), MAX()**: Fundamental for aggregating or summarizing data.
    - **ROUND()**: Use to present outputs clearly. *Example*: =ROUND((C3*C4),2) ensures a ratio or rate displays only two decimals.
2. **Financial Functions**
    - **NPV()**: Calculates the Net Present Value of future cash flows.
        - *Example*: =NPV(Discount_Rate, CashFlow_Range).
    - **IRR()**: Determines the internal rate of return, vital for equity sponsors.
        - *Example*: =IRR(Equity_CashFlows).
    - **PMT()**: Computes periodic loan payments for a given interest rate and term.
        - *Example*: =PMT(Annual_Rate/12, 60, -Principal_Amount) finds monthly payments for a 5-year loan.
3. **Logical Functions**
    - **IF(), AND(), OR()**: Conditionally alter calculations. *Example*: =IF(Debt_Coverage<1.0,"Breach","Healthy").
4. **Lookup and Reference Functions**
    - **VLOOKUP(), HLOOKUP()**: Useful for structured data retrieval.
    - **INDEX() + MATCH()**: More robust than VLOOKUP, especially if columns move or if you need to search multiple fields. *Example*:

Copy code

=INDEX(B2:B10, MATCH(E1, A2:A10, 0))

Essential Tabs for an LBO Model

Assumptions
Central hub for inputs like growth rates and exit multiples.

Financial Statements
Tracks the company's profitability and financial health.

Debt Schedule
Monitors principal, interest, and covenants.

Outputs
Highlights key metrics like IRR, MOIC, and sensitivity results.

This organization ensures clarity and facilitates collaboration in LBO modeling.

2.2 Data Analysis Tools

1. **Pivot Tables**
   - Summarize historical or projected data (e.g., dissecting revenue by product line or region).
   - Quickly pivot data to reveal trends or outliers.
2. **What-If Analysis**
   - **Goal Seek**: Solve for a single variable to reach a target outcome (e.g., "What growth rate is needed for a 25% IRR?").
   - **Scenario Manager**: Save multiple sets of assumptions (Base, Upside, Downside) and toggle among them.
   - **Data Tables**: Generate sensitivity grids showing how changes in two variables (e.g., entry multiple and exit multiple) affect IRR.

2.3 Keyboard Shortcuts (Quick Reference)

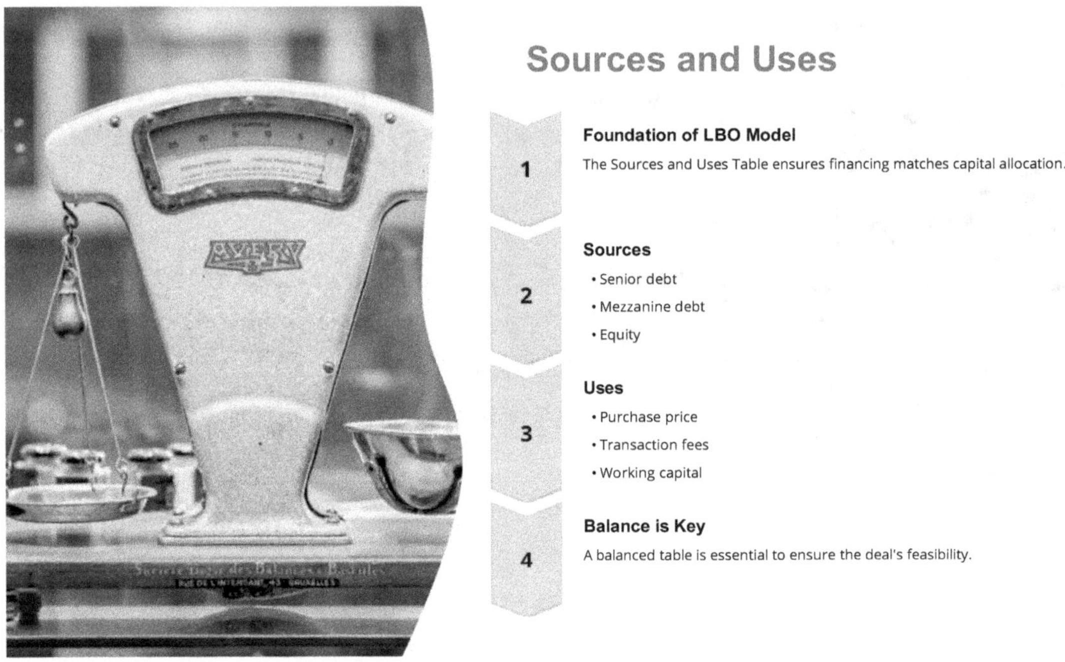

Shortcut	Action
Ctrl + Shift + L	Toggle filters
Ctrl + T	Convert a cell range into a formatted Table
Alt + E + S + V	Paste Special → Values only
Ctrl + R	Fill cells to the right
Ctrl + Shift + "+"	Insert cells or rows (depending on selection)
Ctrl + [/ Ctrl +]	Trace precedents / dependents (for formula auditing)

3. Structuring an LBO Model in Excel

A **user-friendly** LBO model organizes inputs, calculations, and outputs in separate tabs, allowing for both efficient data entry and straightforward review.

3.1 Recommended Tab Layout

Tab	Content	Purpose
Assumptions	Growth rates, interest rates, exit multiples, tax rates, etc.	Central hub for all key variables—adjust here to drive entire model
Income Statement	Projected revenues, costs, EBITDA, net income	Tracks profitability over the LBO horizon (5–7 years typically)
Balance Sheet	Assets, liabilities, equity breakdown	Ensures that the company's financial position remains consistent
Cash Flow	Operating, investing, financing cash flows	Highlights liquidity, debt repayment capacity, and free cash flow
Debt Schedule	Principal balances, interest calculations, covenants, & amortization	Monitors leverage ratios, interest coverage, and compliance with terms
Output / Summary	IRR, MOIC (multiple on invested capital), DSCR, charts, scenario outputs	Provides immediate visibility into deal feasibility and sponsor returns

Pro Tip: Insert an "Index" or "Navigation" tab at the front, listing all sheet names with hyperlinks. This is especially useful in large or complex models.

3.2 Building Key Components

1. **Sources and Uses Table**
   - **Sources**: Details all forms of financing (e.g., Senior Debt, Subordinated Debt, Sponsor Equity).
   - **Uses**: Allocates capital to purchase price, fees, working capital injections, etc.
   - **Formula Example**:

java

Copy code

Total Uses = Purchase_Price + Transaction_Fees + Working_Capital

Total Sources = Senior_Debt + Mezz_Debt + Equity_Contribution

Ensure ***Total Uses = Total Sources*** *for balance.*

2. **Financial Projections**
   - **Top-Line Revenues**: Link these to assumptions for organic growth or market expansion.
   - **Operating Expenses**: Break out direct costs (COGS) and overhead (SG&A).
   - **EBITDA**: A key measure of operating performance in LBOs.
   - **Net Income**: Incorporate interest expense from the Debt Schedule.
3. **Debt Schedule**
   - **Multiple Tranches**: Senior secured loans, mezzanine financing, high-yield bonds. Track each separately for principal balances, interest calculations, mandatory amortization, bullet payments, and optional prepayments.
   - **Covenant Calculations**: Include lines for total debt/EBITDA and interest coverage (EBITDA/Interest Expense). If any ratio breaches a preset threshold, flag it visually (e.g., conditional formatting in red).
4. **Return Metrics (Output Tab)**
   - **IRR()**: Calculate the sponsor's IRR based on equity flows—initial outflow at close, any interim dividends, and final proceeds upon exit.

- **Cash-on-Cash Multiple (MOIC)**: (Total Equity Proceeds / Initial Equity Investment).
- **DSCR (Debt Service Coverage Ratio)**: EBITDA / (Principal + Interest Payments), vital for showing lenders the company's capacity to meet obligations.

Core Excel Tools for LBO Models

Financial Functions

IRR(), NPV(), and PMT() are vital for returns and debt analysis.

Logical Functions

IF() and AND() manage conditional outputs like covenant breaches.

What-If Analysis

Goal Seek and Data Tables enable scenario testing.

4. Advanced Excel Techniques

4.1 Scenario Analysis

1. **Data Tables**
   - Create a 2D table showing how IRR changes with different exit multiples (horizontal axis) and growth rates (vertical axis).
   - Highlight critical zones (e.g., IRR < 15%) in red to illustrate where the deal becomes less attractive.
2. **Dynamic Charts**
   - Link chart data ranges to named ranges that update automatically when you adjust assumptions.
   - Offer multiple "views" (Base Case, Upside, Downside) at a single click, letting stakeholders see how the model reacts in real time.

4.2 Error Checking

1. **Formula Auditing**
   - **Trace Precedents/Dependents (Ctrl + [/ Ctrl +])**: Follow data flows across sheets to isolate errors quickly.
   - **Evaluate Formula**: Step through complex formulas to see how Excel interprets them.
2. **Circular References**
   - LBO models often face circular references when interest expense depends on average debt balances, which in turn depend on free cash flow. If unavoidable, enable "iterative calculations" and set a low iteration threshold to avoid model instability.

Scenario Analysis for Better Decision-Making

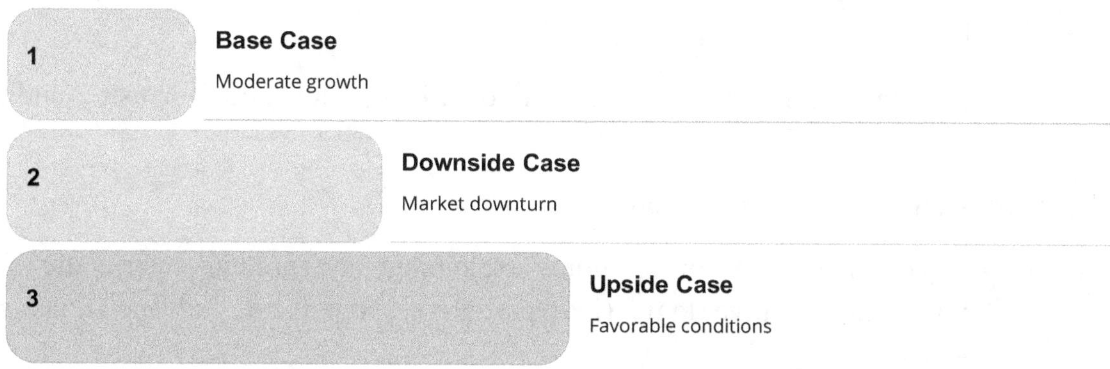

Dynamic scenario analysis enhances decision -making by simulating multiple outcomes. Create 2D sensitivity tables to analyze how changes in variables affect IRR and profitability.

4.3 Macros and Automation

1. **VBA for Repetitive Tasks**
   - Automate tasks like clearing old data, formatting input cells, or generating scenario outputs.
   - *Example Macro*:

vb

Copy code

```
Sub ClearOldData()
  Sheets("Output").Range("B2:B20").ClearContents
End Sub
```

2. **Advanced Scenario Testing**
   - Write macros that systematically vary two or more assumptions (e.g., exit multiple, revenue growth, margin expansion) and store the resulting IRR or DSCR in a separate summary sheet.

5. Tips and Best Practices

1. **Simplicity Wherever Possible**
   - A model with *thousands* of lines can be unwieldy. Focus on the 20% of drivers that cause 80% of outcomes.
   - If you need more detail, consider modularizing your model or using additional supporting schedules.
2. **Transparency and Documentation**
   - Add comment boxes or footnotes explaining key formulas, especially if they contain less intuitive logic (like partial-year interest or advanced tax shield calculations).
   - Keep a "Notes" sheet for major assumptions or changes made during model updates.
3. **Stress Testing**
   - Always run worst-case scenarios (e.g., recession, rising interest rates) to verify covenant compliance and liquidity.
   - Evaluate if the sponsor's IRR remains acceptable under mild or moderate downturns.
4. **Backward Compatibility and Collaboration**
   - Not all team members might have the newest Excel version. Save in a format that maintains essential functionality.
   - If collaborating in real-time, services like SharePoint or OneDrive let multiple users work concurrently. Just be wary of overwriting each other's changes.

6. Common Pitfalls and Troubleshooting

1. **Overcomplicating Models with Minuscule Details**
   - Resist the urge to incorporate every tiny variable. Over-detailing can obscure the big picture and slow performance.
2. **Hardcoded Numbers in Calculations**
   - Always reference assumption cells instead of typing numbers directly into formulas. This approach reduces hidden traps and fosters quick scenario changes.
3. **Ignoring Error Warnings**
   - Never dismiss #REF! or #DIV/0! errors—they often cascade into bigger problems. Investigate and resolve them immediately.
4. **Lack of a Consistent Process for Updates**
   - Ad hoc changes without documentation can lead to confusion. Establish a structured approach:
     1. Update assumptions
     2. Validate formulas and references
     3. Check key outputs
     4. Save a new version

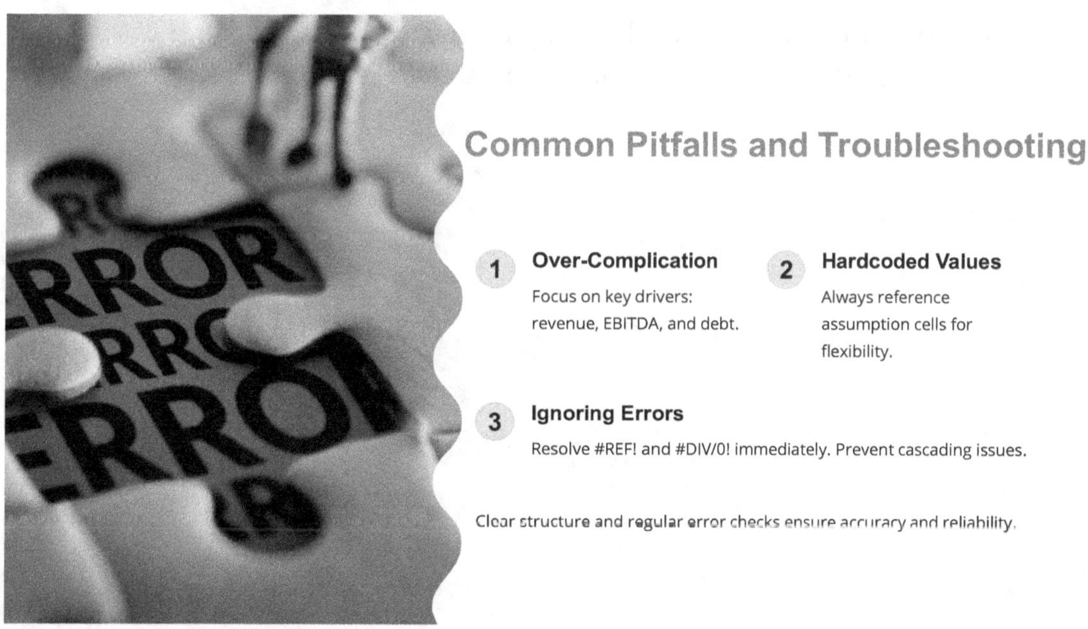

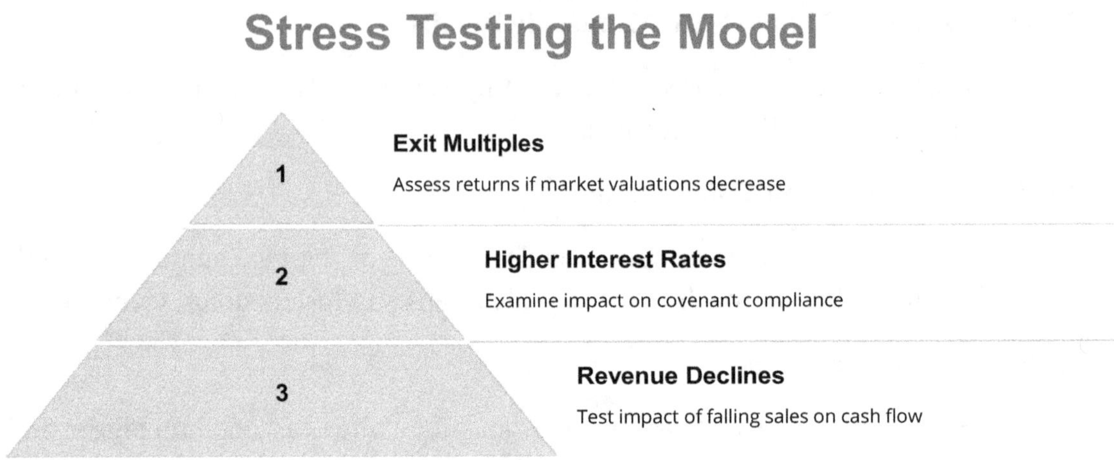

Stress testing evaluates a model's resilience under adverse conditions. It ensures the LBO remains viable across different scenarios.

Conclusion

Excel is a **cornerstone** of leveraged buyout modeling, balancing **technical depth** with **user-friendly** design. By mastering core functions, structuring your workbook intelligently, and harnessing advanced tools like scenario analysis and macros, you can produce an **accurate**, **flexible**, and **insightful** LBO model. Regular stress testing and version control ensure your model remains reliable, even as market conditions and deal parameters evolve.

References and Further Reading

1. **Walkenbach, J. (2015).** *Excel 2016 Bible.* Wiley.
2. **Rosenbaum, J., & Pearl, J. (2020).** *Investment Banking: Valuation, Leveraged Buyouts, and Mergers & Acquisitions.* Wiley.
3. **Damodaran, A. (2012).** *Investment Valuation.* Wiley.
4. **McKinsey & Company. (2021).** *Excel Best Practices for Financial Analysts.*

Advanced Techniques for Flexibility

1

Macros

Automate repetitive tasks like clearing data or running scenarios.

2

Dynamic Charts

Link to data ranges for instant visualization of scenario results.

3

Iterative Calculations

Manage circular references, like interest linked to debt balances.

These advanced tools enhance LBO models, making them both efficient and user -friendly.

Lesson 7: Monte Carlo and Case Study Simulations in LBO Analysis

Lesson Objectives

By the end of this lesson, participants will:

1. **Understand the principles and applications** of Monte Carlo simulations in LBO analysis.
2. **Learn how scenario-based case studies** help evaluate potential risks and opportunities.
3. **Gain expertise in implementing** these techniques in Excel for enhanced decision-making.
4. **Develop strategies to mitigate risks** highlighted by simulations and case studies.

What is Monte Carlo Simulation?

1 **Run Iterations**

Thousands of scenarios with random values

2 **Generate Distribution**

Produce range of possible outcomes

3 **Analyze Probabilities**

Understand likelihood of various results

Monte Carlo simulation helps analysts assess IRR probabilities and debt covenant risks under diverse conditions. It provides a comprehensive view of potential LBO outcomes.

Lesson Content

1. Introduction to Monte Carlo Simulations

Monte Carlo simulations have become a **cornerstone of advanced financial modeling** and risk assessment. In an LBO context—where high leverage amplifies small shifts in operational or financial variables—Monte Carlo helps capture the range of possible outcomes, rather than relying on a single "best guess."

1.1 What is Monte Carlo Simulation?

A Monte Carlo simulation is a computational technique that uses **repeated random sampling** of input variables to generate a **distribution** of potential outcomes. Each iteration represents **one random draw** for each uncertain input (e.g., revenue growth, exit multiples, interest rates), producing a single "run" of how an LBO might unfold.

- **Key Idea**: Instead of one deterministic scenario (e.g., 5% revenue growth every year), Monte Carlo assigns **probability distributions** (e.g., 1–8% growth, centered around 4.5%) and simulates thousands—even tens of thousands—of possible futures.

1.2 Why Use Monte Carlo in LBO Analysis?

Leverage magnifies both returns and risks, so understanding the **probabilistic range** of outcomes is invaluable. Monte Carlo simulations help LBO sponsors and analysts:

1. **Quantify Uncertainty**
    - Instead of a single IRR figure, get a **range** of IRRs and **probabilities** of meeting certain thresholds (e.g., 25% IRR).
2. **Improve Risk Management**
    - Identify extreme "tail" scenarios (like a severe market downturn) that might test debt covenants or threaten liquidity.
3. **Optimize Decision-Making**
    - Adjust capital structure (debt-to-equity ratio) or operational strategies (cost optimization, growth initiatives) based on how different configurations shift the outcome distribution.

Example: If your base-case IRR is 20%, Monte Carlo might reveal a **10% chance** of negative equity returns if revenue growth falls below 2% and margins compress. This insight can shape how you negotiate covenants or plan for contingencies.

2. Structuring Case Study Simulations

While Monte Carlo provides a broad, probabilistic view, **structured scenario analyses** (i.e., case studies) present **targeted, "what-if" snapshots**. These help sponsors deeply examine how certain strategic changes or market conditions affect the deal.

2.1 Why Scenario Analysis?

1. **Holistic Perspective**
    - Deterministic models often fix variables at single-point estimates. Scenario analysis tests multiple sets of assumptions—revealing what happens if, for instance, the target's new product launch is delayed or competitor pressure intensifies.
2. **Stress Testing**
    - Evaluate how robust an LBO is under adverse conditions. For instance, can the company still service debt if EBITDA margins drop from 12% to 9%?
3. **Strategic Planning**
    - By analyzing different "worlds," sponsors can decide if the extra cost of mezzanine financing is worth the risk buffer it provides or if investing more in R&D could mitigate future revenue volatility.

2.2 Structuring Scenarios

Scenario	Revenue Growth	EBITDA Margin	Exit Multiple
Base Case	5%	12%	8x
Upside Case	8%	14%	9x
Downside Case	2%	10%	6x

- **Base Case**:
  - Grounded in historical data and normal industry trends. Assumes stable economic conditions, modest operational improvements.
- **Upside Case**:
  - Reflects above-average performance (e.g., successful product expansions, cost efficiencies).
  - Often used to gauge the **best possible outcome** if all goes well.
- **Downside Case**:
  - Models subdued performance (e.g., 2% revenue growth, 10% margin).
  - **Stress-tests** the LBO structure to see if it can weather lower cash flows.

Pro Tip: More nuanced scenario analyses might include "Mid-Down" or "Mid-Up" layers, or incorporate specific events (e.g., supply chain disruptions, interest rate spikes).

3. Implementing Simulations in Excel

While specialized software (e.g., Crystal Ball, @RISK) can automate Monte Carlo, Excel remains the **most accessible platform**. With basic functions, add-ins, or VBA macros, you can replicate random sampling, link results to your LBO model, and visualize distributions.

3.1 Step-by-Step Monte Carlo Simulation

1. **Setting Up the Model**
   - **Identify Input Variables**: Each variable (e.g., revenue growth, exit multiple) gets a probability distribution—commonly normal, triangular, or uniform.
   - **Assign Ranges/Means**: For example, revenue growth might have a **mean of 5%** and a **standard deviation of 2%**.
   - **Use RAND()** to draw random values.
     - *Example:*

less

Copy code

=NORM.INV(RAND(), Mean, StdDev)

This formula uses the inverse of the normal distribution to generate random draws for each iteration.

2. **Linking to Outputs**
   - Integrate these random draws into your LBO model's revenue lines, cost assumptions, or exit valuations.
   - *Example:* Revenue = Prior_Year_Revenue * (1 + Growth_Rate_Draw)
3. **Running Simulations**
   - **Manual Approach**: Press F9 multiple times to recalc the workbook, capturing results in a separate table.
   - **Macros**: Write a VBA script that loops, say, **5,000 times**, storing IRR results in a column for histogram creation.
4. **Analyzing Results**
   - Build histograms (using Excel's built-in chart tools or pivot tables) to see the distribution of IRRs.

- Calculate probabilities: “What % of trials exceed 20% IRR?”
- Identify tail outcomes: The worst 5% of runs might yield <5% IRR or negative returns.

Example of Monte Carlo in LBO Analysis

20%
Base-case IRR
Initial expected return on investment

10%
Risk of Loss
Probability of negative returns

2%
Growth Threshold
Minimum revenue growth needed

Monte Carlo simulation reveals potential risks in LBO scenarios. It highlights the need for contingency planning.

1. **Renegotiate Debt Covenants**

2. **Incorporate More Equity**

3. **Reduce Risk Exposure**

3.2 Implementing Scenario Analysis in Excel

1. **Define Variables**
   - Hardcode or link references for each scenario's assumptions (revenue growth, margin, multiple).
2. **Simulate Outcomes**
   - Connect these scenario assumptions to the LBO model.
   - Use **NPV()** or **IRR()** for returns calculations.
3. **Analyze Outputs**
   - Summarize results in a **Scenario Manager** or a side-by-side table.
   - Visualize differences using bar charts or a "tornado chart" that highlights which assumption drives the largest IRR swing.

Scenario Analysis Overview

Scenario analysis complements Monte Carlo by exploring specific "what -if" situations. It evaluates LBO performance under distinct conditions, providing targeted insights into deal resilience.

4. Risk Management in Simulations

Whether using Monte Carlo or scenario analysis, the goal is to uncover how an LBO might fail—and how to **pre-empt or cushion** that failure.

4.1 Key Risks in LBO Transactions

1. **Financial Risks**
   - **Over-leverage**: High debt amplifies downside if cash flow lags.
   - **Interest Rate Fluctuations**: Rising rates can spike interest expense, straining coverage ratios.
2. **Operational Risks**
   - **Underperformance**: Failing to hit growth or cost synergy targets.
   - **Management Execution**: Lack of expertise or misalignment with sponsor goals can stifle improvements.
3. **Market Risks**
   - **Economic Downturns**: Reduced consumer demand or investment appetite.
   - **Valuation Compression**: Lower exit multiples if overall market sentiment worsens.

4.2 Mitigation Strategies

Risk	Mitigation Strategy	Example
Interest Rate Risk	Hedge with swaps or caps	Lock in fixed interest rates for a portion of debt
Revenue Shortfalls	Diversify or pivot products	Expand into new geographies or product lines
Exit Valuation Risk	Operational improvements	Boost EBITDA to partially offset a lower multiple
Supply Chain Disruption	Dual sourcing, inventory mgmt	Maintain secondary suppliers; optimize stock levels

Risk Management in LBO Simulations

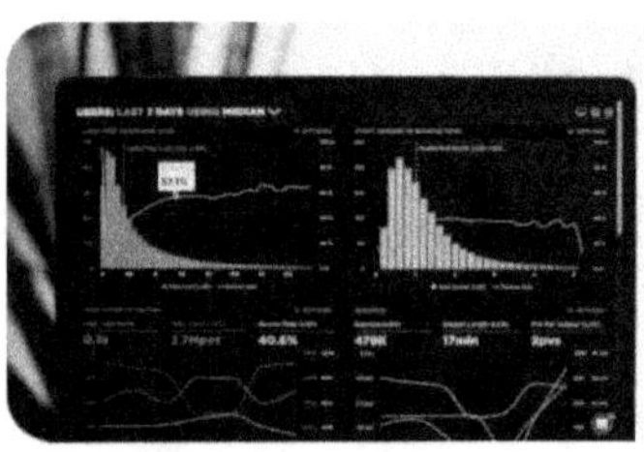

Risk Identification

Monte Carlo and scenario analysis highlight risks like over-leverage and interest rate spikes.

Mitigation Strategies

Implement hedging, revenue diversification, and flexible debt structures to ensure resilience.

Proactive Measures

Anticipate and prepare for adverse conditions to maintain LBO stability.

Pro Tip: Always ensure **covenant headroom** (e.g., a leverage ratio that remains well below thresholds in downside scenarios). This flexibility can save a deal from technical default if macro conditions worsen.

5. Case Study: Simulating an LBO for "RetailCo"

Let's illustrate how Monte Carlo and scenario-based approaches combine in a **realistic** example.

5.1 Background

- **Target**: RetailCo, a mid-sized specialty retailer.
- **Transaction Value**: $800 million
- **Capital Structure**:
    - Senior Debt: $400 million
    - Mezzanine Debt: $200 million
    - Sponsor Equity: $200 million

5.2 Simulation Setup

1. **Input Variables**
    - **Revenue Growth**: 1–8% (normal distribution, mean ~4.5%, std dev ~2%)
    - **EBITDA Margin**: 10–14% (uniform distribution)
    - **Exit Multiple**: 6–10x (triangular distribution, peak at 8x)
2. **Monte Carlo Execution**
    - **10,000 Iterations**: Each iteration draws random values for these variables.
    - **Output**: IRR, DSCR, probability of covenant breach.
3. **Scenario Overlay**
    - **Base Case**: (5% growth, 12% margin, 8x exit)
    - **Downside Case**: (2% growth, 10% margin, 6x exit)
    - **Upside Case**: (8% growth, 14% margin, 9x exit)

5.3 Results and Insights

Metric	Base Case	Downside Case	Upside Case
Revenue Growth	5%	2%	8%
EBITDA Margin	12%	10%	14%
Exit Multiple	8x	6x	9x
IRR	25%	15%	35%

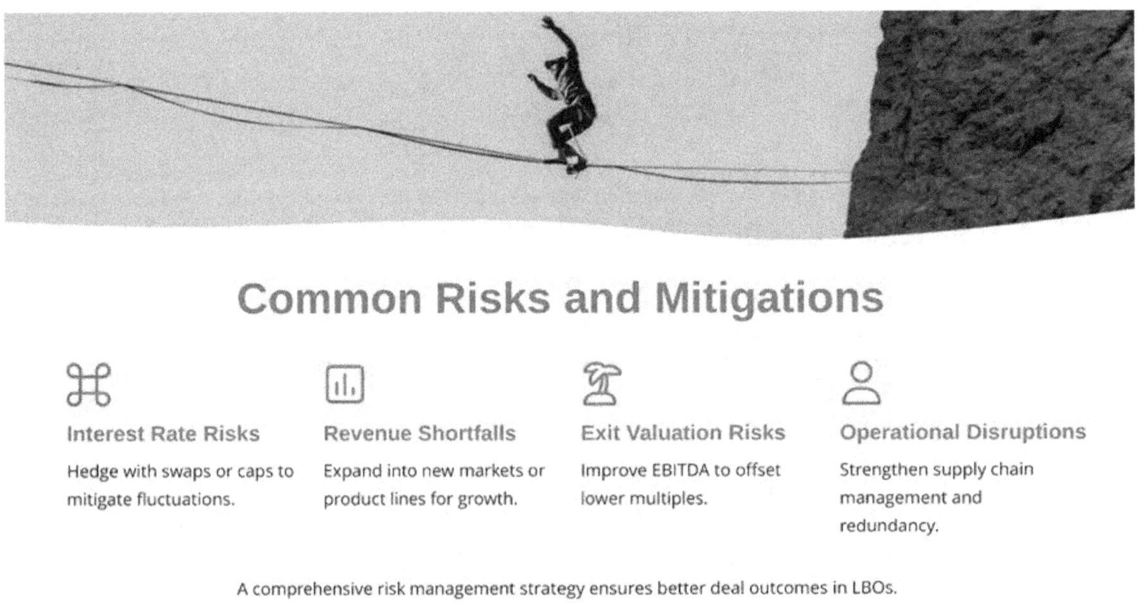

- **Monte Carlo**: Simulation showed a 70% probability that IRR exceeds 20%, but a 10% chance IRR falls below 10%.
- **Downside**: Not catastrophic, but enough to threaten near-term covenants if margins slip below 10%.
- **Recommended Strategies**: Sponsor might negotiate a **covenant-lite structure** or ensure an extended tenor on mezzanine debt to reduce refinancing risk.

Self-Study Questions

1. **Explain how Monte Carlo simulations differ** from deterministic models in LBO analysis. Which advantages do they offer in capturing risk?
2. **Design a scenario analysis structure** for a hypothetical technology firm LBO. What key assumptions would you vary, and why?
3. **Identify key risks** in LBO transactions (financial, operational, market) and propose at least one **mitigation strategy** for each.
4. **Outline the steps for creating** a Monte Carlo simulation in Excel for revenue growth. Which formulas or add-ins would you use?
5. **Evaluate the impact of downside scenarios** on LBO outcomes. How might sponsors **adapt** financing structures or operational plans to manage these risks?

Scenario Analysis in Excel

1. **Use Excel Tools**
   Utilize Scenario Manager or Data Tables for analysis.
2. **Simulate Changes**
   Model impacts of varying growth rates and margins on outcomes.
3. **Calculate Key Metrics**
   Determine effects on IRR or DSCR.
4. **Visualize Results**
   Create bar charts or tornado charts for clear stakeholder communication.

Lesson Takeaways

1. **Monte Carlo Simulations**: Offer a **probabilistic** view of outcomes, highlighting not just the average IRR but the full distribution of possible returns.
2. **Scenario-Based Case Studies**: Provide **structured "what-if" analyses**, enabling sponsors to stress-test and refine assumptions about revenue, margins, and exit multiples.
3. **Excel Tools**: Built-in functions, add-ins (like @RISK), and VBA can automate thousands of iterations, producing histograms, probabilities, and sensitivity analyses.
4. **Risk Management**: Simulations reveal vulnerabilities—such as over-leverage or operational fragility—allowing preemptive strategies (hedges, diversification, covenant negotiations).
5. **Practical Application**: Combining Monte Carlo's broad distribution perspective with scenario analysis's deeper insights can lead to more robust **decision-making** and better **contingency planning**.

Implementing Monte Carlo Simulations in Excel

1. **Random Sampling**

   Use Excel functions like RAND() for variables such as growth rates or exit multiples.

2. **Function Combination**

   Combine RAND(), NORM.INV(), and VBA macros to generate thousands of iterations.

3. **Result Visualization**

   Summarize results in histograms or tables for easy risk and probability analysis.

References and Further Reading

1. **Glasserman, P. (2004).** *Monte Carlo Methods in Financial Engineering.* Springer.
2. **Pindyck, R. S., & Rubinfeld, D. L. (2012).** *Microeconomics: Advanced Applications.* Pearson.
3. **McKinsey & Company. (2021).** *Risk Management in Private Equity: Tools and Techniques.*
4. **Teten, D. (2022).** *How Private Equity Firms Manage Market Risks.* Journal of Finance.
5. **Bain & Company. (2022).** *Global Private Equity Report: Risk and Resilience.*

Lesson 8: Leveraging Data Tools in LBO Analysis

Lesson Objectives

By the end of this lesson, participants will:

1. **Understand the critical role of data platforms** (e.g., Bloomberg, Reuters Thomson, FactSet, Capital IQ) in LBO analysis.
2. **Learn how to use data tools** for precedent transaction analysis and comparable company analysis (comps).
3. **Leverage real-time data** for dynamic decision-making in LBO structuring and valuation.
4. **Integrate data platforms into Excel models** for efficient, accurate, and up-to-date analysis.

Why Use Data Tools?

Market Intelligence

Data tools provide access to vast amounts of market data, allowing analysts to gain deeper insights into industry trends, competitor activities, and macroeconomic conditions.

Benchmarking Capabilities

Compare your target company against its peers using comprehensive data sets that include financial metrics, market share, and valuation multiples.

Risk Assessment Metrics

Data tools help quantify and monitor potential risks associated with an LBO, such as credit risk, operational risk, and regulatory risk.

Lesson Content

1. Introduction to Data Tools in LBOs

Modern LBO transactions demand **rapid access** to large volumes of financial, market, and industry-specific data. Data platforms such as **Bloomberg**, **Reuters Thomson**, **FactSet**, and **Capital IQ** deliver this intelligence in **real time** or with minimal delay, helping you benchmark valuations, gauge market appetite, and fine-tune capital structures.

1.1 Why Use Data Tools?

1. **Comprehensive Market Intelligence**
    - Quickly evaluate historical and real-time financial data to spot trends, price acquisitions, or refine assumptions about cost of capital.
    - **Example**: Use FactSet to pull 10-year financial histories for potential targets and identify patterns in revenue growth or margin expansion.
2. **Benchmarking and Comparables**
    - Derive valuation benchmarks by analyzing **precedent transactions** in the same sector or region.
    - **Example**: Capital IQ can filter deals by industry, deal size, geography, and enterprise value, letting you see typical EV/EBITDA multiples or debt structures in recent LBOs.
3. **Risk Assessment**
    - Economic indicators (e.g., interest rates, GDP growth, commodity prices) help you **stress-test** how external factors might impact debt costs or exit multiples.
    - **Example**: Track macro signals (like rising inflation or changes in Fed policy) to anticipate how credit spreads might shift over the investment horizon.

Platform	Strengths	Use Cases
Bloomberg	Real-time data, analytics, broad coverage	Financial modeling, M&A analysis, global news
Reuters	Comprehensive news, macro & market data	Precedent transactions, industry trend analysis
FactSet	Customizable data feeds & analytics	Peer analysis, scenario modeling, portfolio tracking
Capital IQ	Detailed transaction & company data	Valuation benchmarking, financial modeling

Data Tools and Their Strengths

1 Bloomberg

Real-time data, analytics, and global news coverage ideal for financial modeling.

2 Reuters Thomson

Focused on macroeconomic and industry trends for strategic insights.

3 FactSet

Customizable data feeds for scenario modeling and peer analysis.

4 Capital IQ

Offers granular transaction details for precise valuation benchmarking.

2. Precedent Transaction Analysis

Precedent transaction analysis (often called "transaction comps") is pivotal in LBO valuations, as it reveals **actual market prices** paid for comparable companies under similar market conditions.

2.1 What Is Precedent Transaction Analysis?

- **Definition**: Study historical LBO deals (or broader M&A deals, if no direct LBO sample exists) in the same industry or region to gather insights on valuation multiples, capital structures, and transaction premiums.
- **Objective**: Establish a **range** of plausible multiples—EV/EBITDA, debt-to-EBITDA, equity-to-debt ratio—that sponsors and lenders found acceptable in recent deals.

2.2 Using Data Tools for Precedents

1. **Identify Relevant Transactions**
    - Filter transactions by **industry**, **deal size**, **geography**, and timeframe.
    - **Example**: Use Bloomberg's M&A function (MA) to query retail-sector LBOs over the last five years, sorting by date, enterprise value, and sponsor type.
2. **Extract Key Metrics**
    - Pull data on **EV/EBITDA**, **purchase price**, **transaction premium**, **financing mix**, and **leverage ratio**.
    - **Example**: Reuters Thomson might show how many deals used mezzanine debt vs. high-yield bonds, along with their respective interest rates.
3. **Analyze Trends**
    - Examine whether multiples are trending up or down over time, correlated with market cycles or interest rates.
    - Spot structural evolutions (e.g., more covenant-lite loans) or changes in the typical equity contribution.

Case Study—RetailCo Acquisition (2022)

- **Precedent Transactions**: The data points to an **average EV/EBITDA multiple of 7.5x** and a **leverage ratio of ~4.5x** debt-to-EBITDA for retail deals in the mid-market range.
- **Insights**: Suggests that a sponsor targeting a similar transaction multiple is consistent with recent market appetite, and that a 4.5x debt load is not excessive by retail-sector standards.

Metric	Source	Insights
EV/EBITDA Multiples	Bloomberg, Reuters, Capital IQ	Benchmark valuation levels
Leverage Ratios	FactSet, Capital IQ	Assess typical debt structures
Premium Paid	Bloomberg Terminal	Understand competitive dynamics in acquisitions

Precedent Transaction Analysis Overview

1. **Market Trends**
   Precedent transaction analysis offers insights into market trends and valuation multiples.
2. **Similar Deals**
   By studying similar deals, you can gain valuable information about what sponsors and lenders find acceptable under current conditions.
3. **Key Metrics**
   Common metrics used include EV/EBITDA and leverage ratios.

3. Comparable Company Analysis (Comps)

Comparable company analysis ("trading comps") focuses on **publicly traded peers** of the target. It's another cornerstone of LBO valuation because it reveals how the market prices similar businesses in **real-time**.

3.1 What Is Comparable Company Analysis?

- **Definition**: Evaluate the target's valuation metrics (EV/EBITDA, Price-to-Earnings, EV/Sales) against a peer group of similar **public** firms.
- **Objective**: Derive a **valuation range** and gauge investor sentiment around multiples for that industry, size bracket, or region.

3.2 Using Data Tools for Comps

1. **Screen for Comparable Companies**
   - Filter by **industry code** (NAICS, SIC), **market cap**, **revenue range**, or **geographic focus**.
   - **Example**: Bloomberg's EQS (Equity Screening) can display mid-cap software companies with 5-year revenue CAGRs above 10%.
2. **Collect and Standardize Data**
   - Pull metrics like **revenue**, **EBITDA**, **net income**, and **share price**.
   - Adjust for non-recurring expenses or one-time events to keep data consistent across peers.
3. **Calculate Key Ratios**
   - **EV/EBITDA**: A popular multiple for LBO deals because it focuses on cash-generating ability.
   - **P/E** (Price-to-Earnings): Reflects market sentiment on growth prospects, though less relevant for highly leveraged scenarios.
   - **EV/Sales**: Useful in sectors with low or negative EBITDA (like early-stage tech).

Target—TechCo (Mid-Cap Software Firm)

- Comps: EV/EBITDA range of **10x–12x** and a P/E ratio of ~20x among established software peers.
- **Insights**: This range suggests TechCo might command a valuation premium if it's growing faster than the peer group or has superior margins.

Comparable Metric	Description	Application
EV/EBITDA	Enterprise Value to EBITDA ratio	Reflects core operating profitability
P/E	Price-to-Earnings ratio	Indicates investor optimism or skepticism
EV/Sales	Enterprise Value to Sales ratio	Often used for early-stage or high-growth companies

Comparable Company Analysis (Comps) Overview

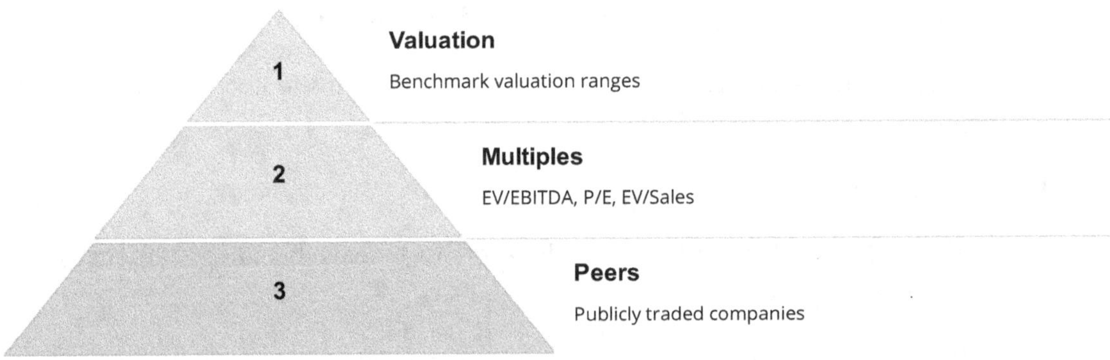

Comparable company analysis evaluates how public peers of a target are valued in the market.

4. Real-Time Data Acquisition

Real-time data can **make or break** an LBO model's accuracy. Market sentiment—and thus interest rates, stock prices, or credit spreads—can shift quickly, especially in volatile markets.

4.1 Why Real-Time Data Matters

- **Reduced Risk of Outdated Assumptions**: Basing your financing structure on last month's credit spread could lead to mispriced debt or mismatched interest coverage estimates.
- **Quick Reaction to Volatility**: If equity markets tumble, your **exit multiple** might shrink, prompting a re-evaluation of how much leverage you should take on.

4.2 Using Data Tools for Real-Time Updates

1. **Market Data Feeds**
   - **Bloomberg**: Real-time updates on bond yields, credit default swaps, commodity prices, and interest rates.
   - **FactSet**: Offers intraday quotes and news for public peer stocks.
2. **Economic Indicators**
   - **Reuters Thomson**: Reports on GDP growth, inflation rates, consumer confidence—each can tweak your LBO's revenue or cost assumptions.
   - **Capital IQ**: Tracks industry-level production indices, making it easier to factor in cyclical slowdowns.
3. **Peer Performance**
   - Compare real-time performance metrics of potential comps or targets to see if they beat or miss earnings, change guidance, or face regulatory issues.

Practical Applications:

- **Debt Pricing**: If you notice a sudden **spike in high-yield spreads**, you might revise your interest expense assumption from 7% to 9%.
- **Exit Strategy**: Monitoring live equity market valuations helps refine your assumption about future IPO or strategic sale multiples.

Data Type	Source	Use Case
Interest Rates	Bloomberg Terminal	Update cost of debt in near-real-time
Economic Indicators	Reuters Thomson	Adjust revenue/cost projections
Peer Metrics	Capital IQ, FactSet	Fine-tune comps-based valuation

Using Data Tools for Comps

1. Screen for comparable companies using filters like industry code, market cap, and revenue range.
2. Standardize and calculate key metrics like EV/EBITDA or P/E.
3. Data from Bloomberg and FactSet ensures your analysis captures sector-specific insights.

5. Integrating Data Tools into LBO Models

Bringing data into Excel-based LBO models is the final piece, ensuring your model references **the most current** metrics without manual re-entry.

5.1 Workflow for Data Integration

1. **Data Extraction**
    - Use APIs or direct export functions. **Example**: FactSet's Excel Add-In can pull multiples or financial statements directly into your spreadsheet.
2. **Dynamic Linking**
    - **Bloomberg API** or **Reuters Eikon** Excel plugins automatically refresh quotes or bond yields.
    - Instead of manually typing updated multiples, your model fetches them each morning, flagging any significant changes.
3. **Scenario Planning**
    - With automated data feeds, you can quickly run best-case, base-case, and downside-case scenarios by toggling references to real-time metrics.

Scenario Planning with Data Tools

1 **Best-Case**

Platforms allow sponsors to quickly adjust data inputs to explore best case scenarios.

2 **Base-Case**

Sponsors can easily test the impact of different assumptions on base-case models.

3 **Downside**

Stress-testing models for downside scenarios becomes streamlined with dynamic data.

5.2 Tips for Effective Integration

- **Data Validation**: Cross-check your downloaded data with original sources or alternate platforms. Discrepancies sometimes arise from currency conversions or timing delays.
- **Version Control**: Keep backups of your model (e.g., "LBOModel_v1_Date"), especially before refreshing data. This helps you revert if errors creep in.
- **Automation**: Macros can handle repetitive tasks like refreshing queries, copying new comps data, or updating scenario parameters.

Real-Time Data Applications

1. **Debt Pricing**
   Monitor high-yield spreads to refine cost-of-debt estimates.
2. **Exit Strategy**
   Track equity market movements to adjust valuation multiples.
3. **Platform Integration**
   Platforms like Reuters Thomson and FactSet make these updates seamless.

Example:

A sponsor building a retail LBO model might schedule a **daily macro** that:

1. Pulls updated retail sales growth figures from Capital IQ.
2. Fetches new interest rate data from Bloomberg.
3. Recalculates the model's IRR and DSCR.
4. Emails a summary of changes to the deal team.

Self-Study Questions

1. **Explain the advantages** of using platforms like Bloomberg or FactSet for LBO analysis. Which specific data points are most crucial for structuring an LBO?
2. **Design a precedent transaction analysis** framework for a hypothetical retail acquisition. What filters and metrics would you emphasize in data selection?
3. **How can real-time data** improve decision-making in LBO structuring and valuation? Provide an example of a scenario where outdated data might compromise an LBO.
4. **Identify the key metrics** in comparable company analysis and their relevance to LBO valuation. Why might EV/EBITDA be more important than P/E in certain sectors?
5. **Describe the workflow** for integrating dynamic data feeds into an Excel-based LBO model. What are the main pitfalls to watch for?

Integrating Data into LBO Models

1 **Automated Updates**

Real-time data feeds eliminate manual re -entry.

2 **Dynamic Linking**

APIs connect data sources to key assumptions.

3 **Model Accuracy**

Data integration ensures model alignment with market trends.

Lesson Takeaways

- **Data Platforms**: Tools like Bloomberg, Reuters, FactSet, and Capital IQ give you **comprehensive intelligence**—from historical precedents to real-time market shifts.
- **Precedent Transactions**: Observing how similar deals were priced and structured offers **practical benchmarks** for multiples, leverage, and premiums.
- **Comparable Company Analysis**: Live comps data reveal investor sentiment, letting you calibrate your LBO assumptions around industry-standard valuation multiples.
- **Real-Time Data**: Reduces the risk of basing decisions on stale assumptions; keeps your model aligned with **current** market conditions.
- **Excel Integration**: Automating data feeds and linking them to an LBO model fosters **dynamic**, up-to-date analysis, enhancing both **speed** and **accuracy** in decision-making.

Data Integration Workflow

1. **Extract Data**

   Use APIs or export functions to pull data from financial databases.

2. **Link Dynamically**

   Connect data to LBO model assumptions for dynamic updates.

3. **Automate Updates**

   Use macros to ensure efficiency and accuracy in model updates.

References and Further Reading

1. **Bloomberg L.P. (2022).** *Using Bloomberg for Financial Analysis: A Practitioner's Guide.*
2. **Reuters Thomson (2021).** *Data-Driven Decision Making in Private Equity.*
3. **FactSet Research Systems Inc. (2022).** *Comprehensive Analytics for Investment Professionals.*
4. **Damodaran, A. (2012).** *Investment Valuation: Tools and Techniques for Determining the Value of Any Asset.* Wiley.
5. **Bain & Company (2023).** *Leveraging Market Intelligence in Private Equity.*

Key Tips for Data Integration

Validation

Cross-check downloaded data for accuracy. Validate key assumptions and ensure data integrity.

Version Control

Save backups to prevent loss from errors. Track changes and maintain data consistency.

Automation

Use macros for repetitive tasks like refreshing queries. Optimize efficiency and reduce manual errors.

Lesson 9: Advanced Topics and Future Trends

Lesson Objectives

By the end of this lesson, participants will:

1. **Explore innovations in LBO financing**, including AI-driven models and ESG-linked loans.
2. **Understand the transformative role of technology** in LBO execution and portfolio management.
3. **Identify opportunities and challenges** in emerging markets for LBOs.
4. **Develop strategies** to adapt to global trends in private equity.

Innovations in LBO Financing

1. **Traditional LBO Financing**
   Standard debt structures and manual analytics
2. **Advanced Analytics**
   Data-driven decision making and risk assessment
3. **ESG-Linked Loans**
   Financing tied to sustainability goals
4. **Digital Platforms**
   Streamlined processes and increased flexibility

Lesson Content

1. Innovations in LBO Financing

The financial fabric of leveraged buyouts (LBOs) is rapidly evolving. A confluence of **advanced analytics, sustainability initiatives**, and **regulatory shifts** is reshaping how deals are structured and how returns are generated. Sponsors who adapt to these innovations often secure more flexible, cost-effective, and strategically aligned financing solutions.

1.1 Impact of AI and Data Analytics on Deal Structuring

1. **Enhanced Due Diligence**
    - **AI-Assisted Analysis**: Machine learning algorithms sift through vast quantities of financials, contracts, and operational data at speeds unattainable by human review. This approach uncovers hidden risks—such as underreported liabilities or subtle revenue trends—that might be missed in traditional diligence.
    - **Predictive Risk Identification**: AI can draw correlations between historical performance, industry indicators, and macroeconomic conditions to flag red-flag scenarios (e.g., supply-chain vulnerabilities, upcoming regulatory shifts).
    - **Example**: A private equity firm used a predictive analytics tool to model a target's future cash flows under various pandemic-related supply constraints. Identifying potential revenue dips early led to a 20% discount in the final deal valuation.
2. **Valuation Precision**
    - **Real-Time Market Data**: AI-driven models tap into real-time feeds—covering competitor performance, commodity prices, or credit spreads—to refine discount rates, growth projections, and synergy calculations.
    - **Geopolitical and Seasonality Factors**: Advanced algorithms can account for cyclical events (e.g., holiday sales, harvest seasons) or macro shocks (e.g., tariffs, sanctions) more accurately than static spreadsheets.
    - **Case Study**: A consumer goods company reduced deal-pricing variance by **15%** by leveraging AI insights that incorporated social media sentiment data into demand projections.

3. **Portfolio Optimization**
    - **Asset-Level Insights**: AI and big data methods highlight underperforming segments across a portfolio—pinpointing operational inefficiencies or unproductive SKUs.
    - **Scenario Simulation**: Sponsors can rapidly test how different **debt-to-equity** mixes influence the probability of covenant breaches or required refinancing.
    - **Advanced Divestiture Strategies**: When AI identifies long-term margin decline in a particular brand or product line, sponsors can consider a timely divestiture to reallocate capital into higher-growth assets.

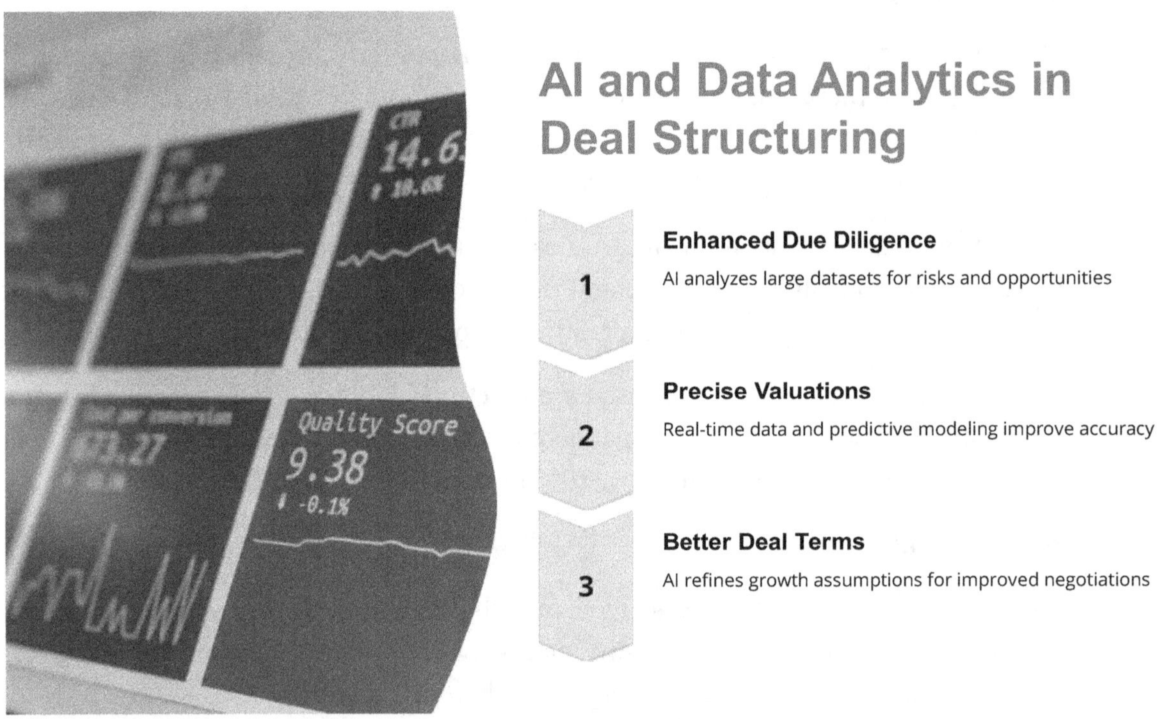

1.2 Evolution of Debt Instruments and Financing Strategies

1. **Unitranche Debt**
    - **Blended Senior and Subordinated Structures**: Merges multiple debt layers into a single tranche, simplifying negotiations and administrative overhead.
    - **Flexibility for Mid-Market**: Especially favored in mid-market LBOs where sponsors seek streamlined financing (one set of covenants, one lender group) without juggling multiple lender classes.
    - **Application**: A mid-sized healthcare acquisition used a $100 million unitranche facility, cutting legal and arrangement fees by 30% compared to a multi-tiered structure.
2. **Sustainability-Linked Loans (SLLs)**
    - **ESG Targets**: Loan terms—particularly interest rates—are tied to meeting **environmental**, **social**, or **governance** milestones.
    - **Reduced Cost of Capital**: If the portfolio company meets these ESG metrics (e.g., carbon footprint reduction, increased board diversity), the interest margin declines.
    - **Example**: A renewable energy firm secured an SLL with a 50-basis-point interest reduction for cutting CO_2 emissions by 30% over three years, aligning shareholder returns with responsible investing.
3. **Digital Syndication Platforms**
    - **Technology-Driven Capital Access**: Online platforms facilitate faster, more transparent syndication processes—matching sponsors with potential lenders or co-investors globally.
    - **Real-Time Visibility**: Sponsors see real-time updates on investor demand and pricing dynamics, enabling more agile decision-making.
    - **Future Direction**: As digital syndication matures, we could see tokenized debt instruments or smart contracts, further streamlining capital-raising processes.

Debt Instrument	Characteristics	Advantages
Unitranche Debt	Single blended senior/subordinated facility	Simplifies structure, lowers transaction costs
Sustainability-Linked Loans	Rates tied to ESG milestones	Aligns financing with responsible investing
Digital Syndication Platforms	Tech-enabled capital syndication	Faster fundraising and transparent pricing

AI-Powered Portfolio Management

Asset Performance Analysis

Leveraging AI to identify underperforming assets and model complex debt-to-equity scenarios

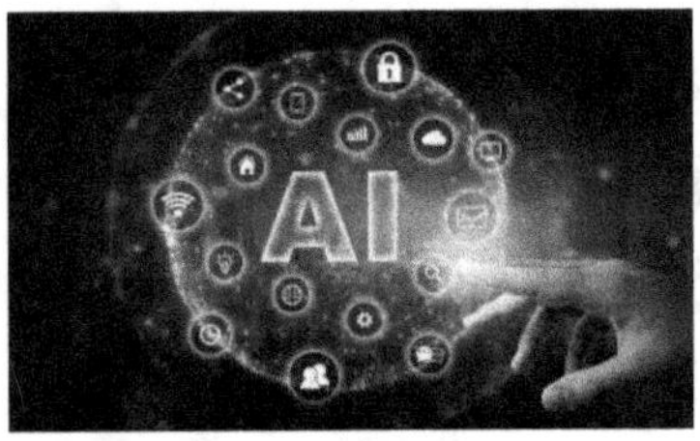

Divestiture Strategies

AI-powered insights enabling precise capital allocation and strategic portfolio management

Operational Improvements

Utilizing artificial intelligence to enhance operational margins across portfolio companies

2. The Role of Technology in LBOs

Beyond financing, technology deeply influences **portfolio management** and **value creation**. From IoT-driven supply chain improvements to advanced cybersecurity measures, sponsors are increasingly depending on digital innovation to boost returns.

2.1 Digital Transformation in Portfolio Companies

1. **Operational Efficiency**
   - **IoT Integration**: Sensors track real-time production throughput, reducing downtime, waste, and inventory mismanagement.
   - **Automation Tools**: RPA (Robotic Process Automation) or robotics can cut labor costs, boost quality control, and minimize errors.
   - **Example**: A manufacturing firm increased plant output by **25%** using robotics for precision assembly, saving $2 million in annual overhead.
2. **Customer-Centric Strategies**
   - **AI-Driven Analytics**: Personalized marketing campaigns can boost conversion and average order value in consumer-facing businesses.
   - **Omnichannel E-Commerce**: Integrating offline and online touchpoints broadens market reach, capturing new revenue streams.
   - **Case Study**: A traditional retail chain doubled its online sales in 12 months by introducing AI-based recommendation engines, capturing a younger digital-savvy demographic.
3. **Cybersecurity Enhancements**
   - **Data Protection**: With increased digitization, threats from hacking, ransomware, or insider breaches multiply. A robust cybersecurity framework is vital to safeguarding IP and consumer data.
   - **Compliance**: Many industries face stringent data privacy regulations (GDPR, CCPA). Failure to comply can result in hefty fines and reputational damage.
   - **Application**: A mid-cap tech portfolio company avoided a **$10M** breach-related cost by proactively upgrading its security protocols.

2.2 Technology-Driven Decision Making

1. **Real-Time Analytics**
   - **Cloud-Based Dashboards**: Centralize data from multiple subsidiaries in a portfolio, offering sponsors or management swift access to KPIs (EBITDA margin, DSO, conversion rates).
   - **Better Insight, Faster Actions**: By spotting a dip in sales or spike in returns early, management can swiftly adjust marketing or supply chain strategies.
2. **Scenario Simulation**
   - **Advanced Modeling**: Tools like predictive AI, Monte Carlo simulations, and digital twins simulate how external market swings (e.g., currency fluctuations, raw material price changes) may impact revenue or cost structures.
   - **Proactive Adjustments**: In a hyper-competitive environment, real-time scenario simulations can guide expansions, cost cuts, or product launches.

Technology Lever	Impact	Example
IoT Devices	Optimizes supply chains	Reduces inventory holding costs by ~20%
AI-Driven Analytics	Enhances customer engagement & segmentation	Increases lifetime value (CLV) by ~15%
Cybersecurity	Protects data & ensures compliance	Avoids fines/breaches; fosters customer trust

3. Emerging Markets and Globalization

Emerging markets present **substantial growth opportunities** but also carry unique risks—**regulatory ambiguity, currency volatility, cultural differences**—that can undermine an LBO if not well managed.

3.1 LBO Opportunities in Emerging Economies

1. **Untapped Sectors**
    - **Renewable Energy & Infrastructure**: As governments prioritize clean energy and modernization, private equity can fund wind farms, solar fields, or critical transport/logistics infrastructure.
    - **Healthcare & Pharma**: Rapidly growing populations need better healthcare, pharmaceuticals, and telemedicine solutions—fertile ground for LBO-driven consolidation.
    - **Tech & Consumer Services**: Rising middle classes in regions like Southeast Asia and Africa are adopting digital solutions at an accelerated pace.
2. **Family-Owned Businesses**
    - **Succession Planning**: In many emerging markets, decades-old family firms seek external expertise and capital to transition leadership. LBO structures can facilitate a partial or phased owner exit.
    - **Application**: A Latin American retail conglomerate accepted an LBO that introduced professional management while allowing family members to retain board seats and partial equity.
3. **Privatization Initiatives**
    - **State-Owned Enterprises**: Governments privatize to boost efficiency, reduce public debt, or encourage foreign investment.
    - **Case Study**: A Southeast Asian logistics firm, previously government-run, improved EBITDA by **40%** post-privatization, offering sponsors a robust IRR once operational inefficiencies were removed.

3.2 Challenges and Mitigation Strategies

Emerging Market Factor	Challenge	Mitigation Strategy
Regulatory Complexity	Inconsistent legal frameworks	Engage local advisors; invest in compliance & legal counsel
Currency Risks	Volatile exchange rates	Hedge with derivatives or issue local-currency debt
Cultural Nuances	Aligning sponsor objectives with local stakeholders	Build trust via joint ventures, board representation, or transparent governance

Case Study: Logistics Company in Southeast Asia

- **Challenges**: Fragmented supply chains, multi-country regulatory approvals, and currency mismatch.
- **Strategies**: Implemented digital tracking to unify shipments across borders, negotiated tax incentives with local governments.
- **Results**: EBITDA soared by **35%** in two years; IRR surpassed original forecasts at 28%.

Self-Study Questions

1. **Discuss how AI and data analytics** are transforming LBO financing and deal structuring. Which stages of the deal cycle benefit most from these technological insights?
2. **Explain the advantages and risks** of unitranche debt and sustainability-linked loans in LBOs. Provide examples of situations where one might be preferable to the other.
3. **How can emerging market challenges**, such as currency risks and regulatory complexity, be effectively mitigated? What role do local partnerships play in success?
4. **Design a technology-driven strategy** for enhancing operational efficiency in a newly acquired portfolio company (e.g., using IoT, AI, or e-commerce tools).
5. **Evaluate the role of privatization initiatives** in driving LBO opportunities in emerging markets. How do sponsors balance public scrutiny with profitability goals?

Cybersecurity and Compliance

Lesson Takeaways

- **Innovations in Financing**: AI-driven insights, sustainability-linked loans, and digital syndication are reshaping how deals are funded—offering both cost savings and strategic advantages.
- **Technology as a Value Driver**: Operational efficiency, customer engagement, and risk mitigation all benefit from digital tools—be it IoT sensors or advanced cybersecurity.
- **Emerging Markets**: High potential returns, but sponsors must master local regulations, currency hedging, and cultural alignment to succeed.
- **Global Adaptation**: Staying nimble and informed about global trends—like ESG mandates or shifting macro conditions—helps private equity sponsors remain competitive and seize new LBO opportunities.

Technology-Driven Decision Making

1. **Cloud-Based Dashboards**
   Centralized data access across portfolios
2. **Advanced Simulation Tools**
   Monte Carlo models and digital twins for scenario analysis
3. **Real-Time Analytics**
   Faster and more informed decision -making

References and Further Reading

1. **Bain & Company (2023).** *Global Private Equity Outlook: Emerging Markets and Technology.*
2. **McKinsey & Company (2022).** *The Future of Financing in Private Equity.*
3. **Damodaran, A. (2018).** *Valuation in Emerging Markets: Tools and Techniques.* Wiley.
4. **PwC (2022).** *Harnessing AI in Private Equity: Insights and Case Studies.*
5. **Harvard Business Review (2023).** *ESG and the Future of Private Equity Financing.*

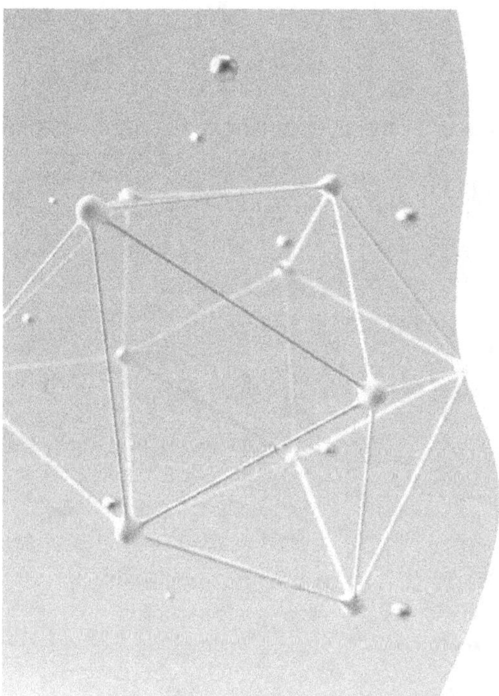

Future Trends in Technology

Tokenized Debt

Blockchain-based instruments for increased liquidity

AI-Driven Tools

Advanced analytics for deal sourcing and management

IoT Integration

Real-time data access redefining agility in private equity

Cybersecurity Protocols

Enhanced digital safeguards for secure transaction environments

Lesson 10: AI-Driven Innovations in LBO Analysis

Lesson Objectives

By the end of this lesson, participants will:

1. **Explore how AI transforms** deal sourcing, financial modeling, and post-acquisition monitoring in LBOs.
2. **Understand the applications** of AI tools for predictive analytics, risk management, and operational optimization.
3. **Learn how to integrate AI-driven strategies** into the LBO lifecycle to enhance decision-making and efficiency.
4. **Evaluate challenges in AI adoption** and implement best practices for successful integration.

Why Use AI in LBO Analysis?

Enhanced Decision-Making

AI processes massive datasets to uncover trends and forecast outcomes.

Efficiency Gains

Automates repetitive tasks, allowing teams to focus on strategic priorities.

Reduced Human Error

Ensures consistency in complex financial models with multiple variables.

Lesson Content

1. Introduction to AI in LBOs

AI is rapidly redefining the **private equity landscape**, helping firms improve speed, accuracy, and insight in every stage of the LBO process. Whether it's **scanning massive data sets** for promising targets or **predicting post-acquisition performance**, AI-driven tools can reduce human bias, cut manual workload, and surface hidden opportunities.

1.1 Why Use AI in LBO Analysis?

1. **Enhanced Decision-Making**
    - **Data-Driven Insights**: AI scrutinizes massive datasets—ranging from financial statements and industry reports to social media sentiment—to identify patterns and forecast potential outcomes.
    - **Real-World Example**: An AI-powered analytics platform might alert sponsors that a consumer goods segment is primed for expansion based on real-time consumer sentiment, macroeconomic trends, and competitor benchmarks.
2. **Efficiency Gains**
    - **Process Automation**: Repetitive tasks like data collection, model building, and early-stage due diligence can be automated, **cutting weeks off** traditional transaction timelines.
    - **Cost Savings**: By automating labor-intensive processes, sponsors can reallocate staff to higher-value tasks, such as strategic negotiations or operational improvements.
3. **Improved Accuracy**
    - **Reduced Human Error**: Standardized workflows and AI-based checks lower the risk of manual mistakes in calculations or data transcription.
    - **Consistency at Scale**: In large-scale financial models involving multiple variables, AI ensures inputs remain synchronized and up-to-date.

Key Applications of AI in LBOs

1. **Deal Sourcing**
   Identifies and ranks high-potential targets, expanding the pipeline.

2. **Due Diligence**
   Summarizes complex legal and operational data, flagging key risks.

3. **Predictive Modeling**
   Ensures better scenario planning for informed decision -making.

4. **Post-Acquisition Monitoring**
   Tracks KPIs to maximize value creation after the deal.

Key AI Applications	Purpose	Impact
Deal Sourcing & Analysis	Identify and rank high-potential targets	Expands pipeline; better strategic alignment
Due Diligence Automation	Summarize legal, financial, operational data	Speeds up analysis; reduces oversight
Predictive Modeling	Forecast financial outcomes	Strengthens scenario planning and valuation
Post-Acquisition Monitoring	Track KPIs across portfolio companies	Ensures ongoing value creation and risk management

2. AI-Enhanced Deal Sourcing

Deal sourcing represents the first point in the LBO lifecycle where AI can deliver immense value. Instead of relying on traditional networks or manual screening, AI-driven platforms can analyze structured and unstructured data—financials, news articles, social media chatter—to flag companies that match an investor's criteria.

2.1 How AI Transforms Deal Sourcing

1. **Pattern Recognition**
   - **Sector & Financial Metrics**: AI sifts through industry databases, identifies undervalued or high-growth firms, and highlights anomalies (e.g., unusual surge in revenue, overperforming profit margins).
   - **Predictive Indicators**: Past performance, supply chain resilience, and patent filings can be combined to forecast future success.
2. **Sentiment Analysis**
   - **Media & Social Scoring**: By gauging customer reviews, employee sentiment, or broader news coverage, AI can reveal brand perception and market momentum—key for spotting emerging or distressed targets.
   - **Risk & Opportunity**: Negative sentiment might signal deep-rooted challenges but also potential turnaround plays.

2.2 Example Workflow: Renewable Energy Sector

Step	Action	Tool Example
Input Parameters	Define sector (renewable energy), revenue range, EBITDA margin thresholds	Bloomberg GPT, Reuters Thomson AI
Data Analysis	AI scans annual reports, news feeds, patent data	Custom AI-based algorithms
Output	Ranked list of targets with sentiment scores, market traction, and risk assessment	AI-generated portfolio watchlist

AI in Deal Sourcing

Data Analysis

AI analyzes structured and unstructured data to identify patterns in financial metrics.

Predictive Indicators

Flags undervalued or high-growth companies using predictive indicators.

Sentiment Analysis

Assesses market perception from social media, customer reviews, and news coverage.

Case Study

- **Inputs**: Sector = Renewable Energy, Revenue $50M–$500M, EBITDA margin >15%.
- **AI Output**: 10 prospective targets with growth potential, aggregated risk scores, and competitor analyses.
- **Result**: Sponsors saved 3 weeks compared to manual sourcing, with more robust data justifying deeper due diligence on top targets.

3. AI in Due Diligence

Due diligence is traditionally time-consuming and error-prone, requiring thorough reviews of legal documents, financial statements, and operational metrics. AI expedites the process by extracting critical data, summarizing complexities, and flagging red flags before they jeopardize the deal.

3.1 Accelerating the Due Diligence Process

1. **Document Review**
    - **Keyword Extraction & Summaries**: Tools like Kira, Leverton, or NLP-based solutions parse hundreds of pages of contracts, highlighting key clauses—change-of-control provisions, indemnities, exclusivities—that warrant closer attention.
    - **Compliance Checks**: Identify areas of potential legal risk, such as environmental or labor regulation breaches, or undisclosed liabilities hidden in footnotes.
2. **Risk Identification**
    - **Natural Language Processing**: AI can interpret tone and context in internal emails or external communications, revealing potential controversies (e.g., pending lawsuits, IP challenges).
    - **Real-World Example**: A sponsor discovered undisclosed environmental fines by scanning public records with AI-based web scraping, averting a post-acquisition surprise.

AI Tool	Functionality	Benefit
Kira Systems	Contract review, clause extraction	Speeds up legal analysis, reduces manual errors
Leverton AI	Automated document indexing & analysis	Enables quick search for compliance or deal terms
ChatGPT Enterprise	Rapid Q&A on document content	Enhances accessibility and quick referencing

AI in Due Diligence

Contract Analysis

AI tools analyze hundreds of pages, extracting key clauses and provisions.

Risk Detection

Natural language processing detects tone and context, surfacing red flags.

Time Savings

Accelerates the due diligence process, saving weeks of manual work.

Comprehensive Insights

Provides holistic view of company performance and potential risks.

Case Study

- **Traditional Approach**: 500 pages of legal documents might take 3–4 weeks for a legal team to parse fully.
- **AI-Assisted**: Completed in under 3 days, surfacing all critical issues and offering a summarized risk profile.

4. AI-Driven Financial Modeling

Financial modeling lies at the heart of LBO analysis—dictating valuations, capital structures, and IRR forecasts. AI enriches models with real-time data and automates scenario tests, elevating both speed and accuracy.

4.1 Transforming Financial Models with AI

1. **Automated Data Integration**
   - **Live Market Feeds**: Tools can pull updated interest rates, FX rates, commodity prices, and peer multiples from platforms like **Bloomberg** or **FactSet**, ensuring your model stays fresh.
   - **Error Minimization**: Direct data feeds reduce manual copy-paste tasks, minimizing transcription errors.
2. **Scenario Simulations**
   - **Monte Carlo at Scale**: AI can run thousands of Monte Carlo simulations, rapidly varying key inputs like revenue growth or cost of capital to produce distribution graphs of expected IRRs.
   - **Edge Case Discovery**: Instead of focusing on just base, downside, and upside, AI unveils lesser-known tail risks or improbable (but possible) scenarios.
3. **Error Detection**
   - **Cohesiveness Checks**: AI-based auditing can confirm that debt schedules, P&L statements, and working capital assumptions flow logically—highlighting any circular references or inconsistent formulas.

Feature	Example	Outcome
Real-Time Updates	Sync with Bloomberg for live interest rates & multiples	Accurate, up-to-date debt cost assumptions
Automated Sensitivity	100+ variable scenario runs in minutes	Comprehensive risk/return analysis
Model Validation	Flagging circular references or misaligned sums	Bolsters model integrity and investor confidence

AI in Financial Modeling

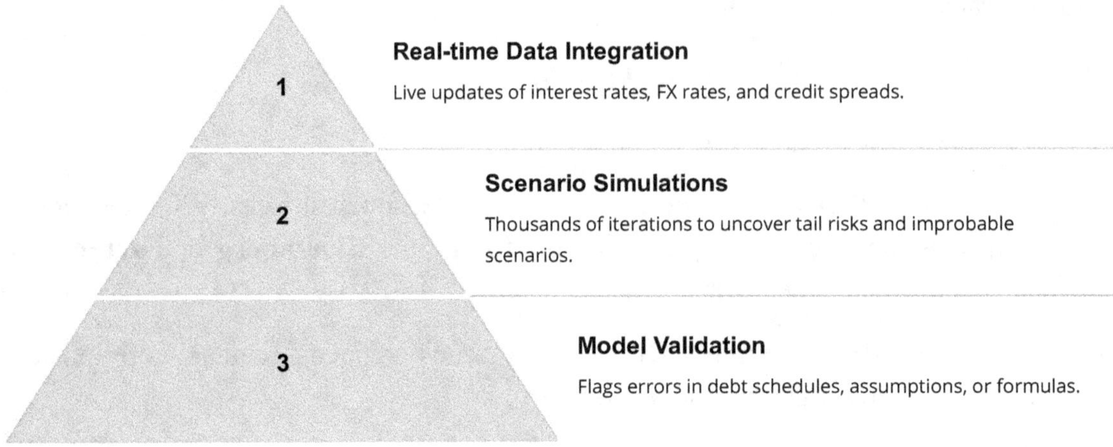

Case Study: Scenario Analysis

- **Setup**:
  - Base: 5% revenue growth, stable margins.
  - Downside: 2% revenue contraction, margin squeeze.
  - Upside: 10% growth, margin expansion.
- **AI Output**: IRR ranges from 12% to 28%, with automated recommendations to trim operational costs under the downside scenario for covenant compliance.

5. AI in Post-Acquisition Monitoring

Value creation doesn't stop at deal closing. AI tools provide continuous monitoring, ensuring sponsors spot early signals—of trouble or opportunity—across their newly acquired portfolio companies.

5.1 Continuous Value Creation

1. **KPI Dashboards**
    - **Cross-Portfolio Aggregation**: Real-time dashboards collate financial and operational metrics (e.g., EBITDA margins, churn rates, production yields) from multiple portfolio companies.
    - **Early Alerts**: If a particular subsidiary's cost of goods sold (COGS) spikes, an AI-based alert can prompt immediate investigation, preventing margin erosion.
2. **Predictive Insights**
    - **Revenue & Demand Forecasting**: AI surfaces patterns (like seasonal buying or influencer-driven spikes) that human analysts might miss.
    - **Cost Optimization**: By analyzing procurement data, an AI might suggest alternative sourcing strategies or renegotiation opportunities with suppliers.
3. **Operational Efficiency**
    - **Root Cause Analysis**: If production line defects surge, AI can correlate machinery logs, shift changes, and supply quality data to isolate the underlying issue.
    - **Real-World Example**: A sponsor saved $1M in annual overhead after an AI tool identified inefficient scheduling practices in a manufacturing plant.

Metric Monitored	AI Insight	Action Taken
Revenue Trends	Identifies declining SKU sales in real time	Adjust marketing or product strategy
Supply Chain Delays	Flags bottlenecks in supplier network	Diversify or renegotiate with new suppliers
Employee Turnover	Predicts attrition hotspots by department	Enhance retention bonuses, training programs

6. Risk Management with AI

In a highly leveraged transaction, **managing risk** is paramount. AI can proactively spot potential pitfalls—whether macroeconomic or operational—enabling sponsors to act before minor issues become deal-breakers.

6.1 Proactive Risk Identification

1. **Market Risks**
   - **Macroeconomic Indicators**: AI constantly monitors GDP forecasts, interest rate shifts, or consumer confidence indices, alerting you if thresholds are crossed (e.g., a sudden interest rate hike that may strain coverage ratios).
2. **Operational Risks**
   - **IoT & Logistics Data**: Real-time feeds from shipping companies or manufacturing lines reveal potential disruptions (e.g., labor strikes, raw material shortages).
   - **Pattern Recognition**: AI might detect cyclical patterns in supply chain breakdowns correlated with weather, trade policy changes, or political unrest.
3. **Financial Risks**
   - **Default Likelihood**: Large volumes of historical credit data allow AI to spot red flags akin to early default warning signs (e.g., negative free cash flow trends, ballooning payables).
   - **Cash Flow Stabilization**: Sponsors can pivot working capital strategies or restructure tranches of debt before liquidity hits a critical low.

6.2 Risk Mitigation Strategies

Risk Type	AI Application	Outcome
Market Risk	Monitor real-time economic indicators	Early strategy pivots (e.g., refinance, hedge)
Operational Risk	Track logistics/production data for anomalies	Avoid supply chain crises, maintain brand reliability
Financial Risk	Identify patterns linked to default or illiquidity	Strengthen cash flow management; reorganize capital structure

Scenario Simulation with AI

1. **Base Case**
   5% revenue growth, stable margins.
2. **Downside Scenario**
   2% revenue contraction.
3. **AI Analysis**
   Calculates IRRs from 12% to 28%.
4. **Recommendation**
   Trim operational costs in downside case for covenant compliance.

7. Challenges and Best Practices in AI Adoption

Despite AI's transformative potential, private equity firms must handle **data quality**, **organizational readiness**, and **ethical considerations**.

1. **Data Quality & Integration**
    - **Inconsistent Data**: Mergers, acquisitions, or varied ERP systems can produce heterogeneous datasets that hinder AI's performance.
    - **Solution**: Standardize data inputs early; invest in robust data warehousing and cleansing processes.
2. **Skill Gaps & Training**
    - **Upskilling Teams**: Analysts and associates need training to interpret AI outputs and incorporate them into strategic decisions.
    - **Domain Knowledge**: AI is most effective when combined with sector-specific expertise (e.g., retail, healthcare, manufacturing).
3. **Ethical & Governance Considerations**
    - **Bias in Algorithms**: Incomplete or skewed datasets can produce biased predictions, leading to suboptimal or unfair decisions.
    - **Regulatory Compliance**: Ensure AI-driven decisions comply with data privacy laws and industry regulations.

Self-Study Questions

1. **Describe how AI enhances** decision-making and efficiency in LBO analysis. Which phases of the LBO lifecycle gain the most from AI-driven insights?
2. **Outline the steps** for implementing AI-driven due diligence in a private equity firm. How do you ensure data quality and reduce model bias?
3. **How can AI tools** be used to optimize financial models and scenario planning for leveraged deals? Provide an example of a multi-scenario IRR forecast.
4. **Evaluate the benefits** of real-time KPI dashboards in post-acquisition monitoring. How do these dashboards aid proactive risk management and operational efficiency?
5. **Identify and discuss strategies** for mitigating financial and operational risks using AI. Where does human oversight remain essential in the risk management loop?

AI in Post-Acquisition Monitoring

Continuous Performance Monitoring

AI tools aggregate KPIs across subsidiaries in real-time.

Trend Identification

Dashboards flag trends like declining sales or rising costs.

Predictive Insights

Help adjust strategies before issues escalate.

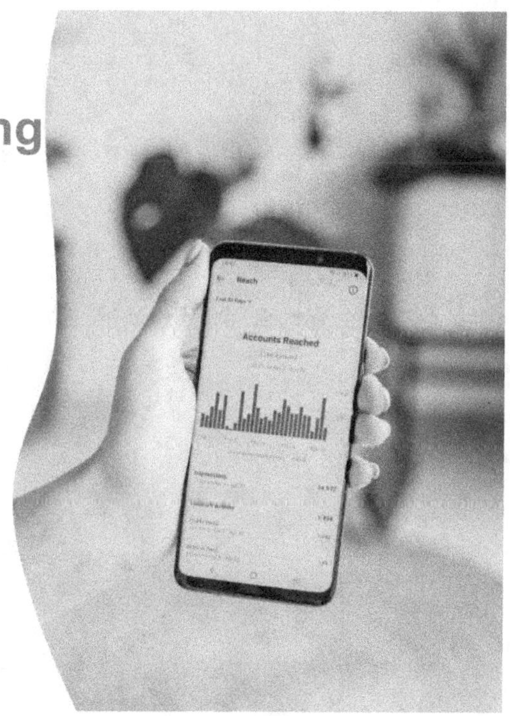

Lesson Takeaways

- **AI Empowers the LBO Lifecycle**: From **deal sourcing** and **due diligence** to **financial modeling** and **portfolio monitoring**, AI injects speed, precision, and forward-looking insights.
- **Predictive Analytics & Dashboards**: Real-time modeling, scenario runs, and KPI tracking foster proactive decisions—crucial in a leveraged environment.
- **Risk Mitigation & Value Creation**: Early red-flag detection, operational fine-tuning, and data-driven synergy identification drive better LBO outcomes.
- **Successful Integration**: High-quality data, effective training, and continuous iteration are core pillars for harnessing AI's full potential in private equity.

Risk Management with AI

Market Risks

Monitors interest rate changes and economic indicators.

Operational Risks

Tracks supply chain disruptions and production inefficiencies.

Financial Risks

Assesses default likelihood and cash flow trends.

References and Further Reading

1. **PwC (2023).** *AI-Driven Innovations in Private Equity.*
2. **Bain & Company (2022).** *Leveraging Technology in Private Equity Operations.*
3. **Damodaran, A. (2021).** *The Future of Valuation: AI and Big Data.* Wiley.
4. **KPMG (2023).** *Harnessing AI for Due Diligence and Financial Modeling.*
5. **McKinsey & Company (2023).** *The Role of AI in Private Equity Transformation.*

Risk Mitigation Strategies

Market Risks

Monitor economic indicators for early pivots like refinancing or hedging.

Operational Risks

Track supply chain data to identify bottlenecks before they escalate.

Financial Risks

Spot patterns tied to defaults, adjust debt or working capital strategies.

Lesson 11: Capstone Project – Comprehensive LBO Simulation

Objective of the Capstone Project

The Capstone Project synthesizes the knowledge and skills acquired throughout this course, providing participants with an **immersive, hands-on** opportunity to apply leveraged buyout (LBO) concepts in a **realistic** (yet simulated) environment. By tackling **three distinct modules**, participants will:

1. **Apply Core Skills**: Use in-depth valuation, financing, structuring, and operational strategies to **execute a hypothetical LBO deal** from start to finish.
2. **Develop Strategic Thinking**: Craft a **detailed plan for value creation** while addressing major risks, challenges, and potential deal breakers.
3. **Refine Communication Abilities**: Present analyses and recommendations in a **professional setting**, simulating an investment committee (IC) meeting where they must defend their assumptions and strategic decisions.

Capstone Project Options

Participants may choose **one** of three project scenarios. Each option has been enhanced with more detail and expanded possibilities so that participants can select an option aligned with **their sector interest** and **career aspirations**. Feel free to **inject your own creative assumptions** (e.g., AI-driven strategies, ESG-linked financing, or emerging market complexities) even beyond the suggested details to deepen your learning.

Case Study Option 1: Retail Turnaround LBO

Input	Details
Background	A struggling retail chain with $1 billion revenue, $100 million EBITDA, and a legacy store network.
Sector	**Retail**, contending with e-commerce disruptions, high operational overhead, and declining foot traffic.
Focus Areas	**E-commerce expansion** and **supply chain optimization** (potential technology solutions, AI-based inventory forecasting).
Key Challenges	Legacy IT systems, **high fixed costs**, limited digital presence, competitive discount retailers.
Potential Value Creation	5% annual revenue growth, +2% EBITDA margin boost (through cost optimization, store closures/relocations, and digital marketing).
Expected Outputs	IRR ~25%; cash-on-cash return ~2.5x; optional synergy from consolidation with existing retail portfolio (if relevant).

Enhanced Scenario Ideas

- **Partnerships or acquisitions** of small direct-to-consumer (DTC) brands to revitalize product offerings.
- **ESG Angle**: Redesign store footprints to be more energy-efficient (lighting, HVAC), leading to possible sustainability-linked financing.
- **AI Approach**: AI-driven demand forecasting to optimize inventory and reduce stock-outs or overstocks.

Case Study Option 2: High-Growth Technology Firm

Input	Details
Background	Mid-cap software firm with \$500M revenue, \$150M EBITDA, specializing in a leading **SaaS** platform.
Sector	**Technology**, focusing on subscription-based solutions with high retention rates.
Focus Areas	**Scaling operations**, entering new markets (global or sector-specific), ramping up R&D for next-gen product lines.
Key Challenges	**Talent acquisition** (competitive tech labor market), sustaining product differentiation against well-funded rivals.
Potential Value Creation	8% annual revenue growth, expanded product suite, deeper market penetration (Asia, Europe), intangible synergy from strategic acquisitions.
Expected Outputs	IRR ~28%; cash-on-cash return ~3x; potentially higher if an IPO exit or strategic sale occurs.

Enhanced Scenario Ideas

- **AI Integration**: Possibly develop an AI module to stay ahead of competing SaaS players, which might shift cost structures and require heavy upfront R&D.
- **Regulatory Hurdles**: Data privacy compliance (GDPR, CCPA) and how that might impact costs or cause legal risk.
- **ESG Angle**: Commit to workforce diversity or green data-center solutions for brand positioning and possible ESG-linked debt.

Case Study Option 3: Emerging Market Logistics Firm

Input	Details
Background	A Southeast Asian logistics provider with $750M revenue, $120M EBITDA, operating in a fragmented, underserved market (rural areas).
Sector	**Logistics**, focusing on last-mile delivery, cross-border trade corridors, and capacity-building via digital transformation.
Focus Areas	**Cost efficiency** (fleet optimization, warehouse automation) and **infrastructure investments** (warehouses, truck fleets).
Key Challenges	Regulatory hurdles, **currency risks** (volatile FX), **fragmented supply chain** with multiple local players and legacy systems.
Potential Value Creation	7% annual revenue growth, improved margins from AI-based route planning, enhanced delivery networks, cross-border e-commerce partnerships.
Expected Outputs	IRR ~26%; cash-on-cash return ~2.8x; optional synergy if the sponsor has existing port or shipping assets in the region.

Enhanced Scenario Ideas

- **Local Partnerships**: JV agreements with postal services or telecom players to gain distribution or data advantages.
- **ESG Angle**: Focus on electric vehicles, carbon-neutral operations, or reducing carbon footprint in the supply chain.
- **AI Approach**: Real-time route optimization, predictive maintenance for vehicle fleets, and advanced demand forecasting across emerging markets.

Project Structure

Module 1: LBO Modeling and Execution

Participants will build a **comprehensive LBO model** for their chosen scenario, incorporating advanced assumptions, multi-scenario planning, and robust sensitivity analysis.

Step-by-Step LBO Modeling (Expanded)

1. **Target Overview**
    - Summarize key operational, market, and financial attributes.
    - Outline any synergy or integration angles (e.g., potential bolt-on acquisitions, cost-cutting synergy, or brand repositioning).
2. **Input Assumptions**
    - **Purchase Price**: Default: 8x EBITDA (adjust as you see fit). Consider real-time comps from similar deals.
    - **Financing Structure**:
        - Senior Debt: $400 million at 5% interest.
        - Mezzanine Debt: $200 million at 10% interest.
        - Sponsor Equity: $200 million.
    - Optional Layer: **Sustainability-linked loan** or a **unitranche** approach.
3. **Sources and Uses Table**

Sources	Amount ($M)	Uses	Amount ($M)
Senior Debt	400	Purchase Price	800
Mezzanine Debt	200	Transaction Fees	10
Sponsor Equity	200	Working Capital	10
Total	**800**	**Total**	**800**

4. **Projections and Assumptions**
    - **Revenue Growth**: Example: 5% base, but incorporate upside/downside variations (2% → 8%).

- **EBITDA Margin**: Example: from 10% to 12% over five years. Factor in cost-savings, synergy, or technology investments.
- **Debt Repayment**: 20% annual senior amortization, mezz bullet, or potential partial refinances.
- **Equity Incentives**: Consider management equity rollovers or earn-outs if relevant.

5. **Key Outputs**
    - **IRR**: Aim for 25%+ over five years (adjust for scenario).
    - **Cash-on-Cash Multiple**: 2.5x target.
    - **DSCR**: Maintain ≥1.5x coverage for lenders' comfort.
    - **Sensitivity & Scenario Analysis**: Evaluate how IRR & DSCR shift if interest rates rise, margins slip, or synergy doesn't materialize as planned.
6. **Scenario Analysis (Hypothetical Example)**

Scenario	Revenue Growth	EBITDA Margin	IRR	Cash-on-Cash
Base Case	5%	12%	25%	2.5x
Downside Case	2%	10%	15%	1.8x
Upside Case	8%	14%	32%	3.2x

Advanced Modeling Suggestions

- Incorporate AI-based revenue or margin forecasts into your model.
- Test **ESG-linked** outcomes, e.g., achieving carbon neutrality within 5 years might trigger a 50bp interest rate discount.
- Explore **refinancing** or **recapitalization** scenarios if growth outperforms.

Module 2: Investment Memo Preparation

Compile a **professional investment memo** summarizing your deal. This memo is akin to what you'd present to a sponsor's Investment Committee or potential co-investors.

Investment Memo Structure

1. **Executive Summary**
    - Clear, 1-page snapshot: target overview, deal thesis, high-level financials (purchase multiple, IRR), key value drivers.
2. **Valuation and Financial Metrics**
    - Outline key assumptions: EV/EBITDA, capital structure, cost of capital.
    - Include 5–7 year forecasts for revenue, EBITDA, leverage ratios.
    - Show scenario-based IRR & cash-on-cash returns.
3. **Strategic Plan**
    - **Operational Improvements**: e.g., cost reductions, store closings, or tech upgrades.
    - **Revenue Growth**: e.g., new product lines, e-commerce expansions, cross-border entry.
    - **Synergy Potential**: if applicable, highlight cost synergy or brand synergy with existing portfolio.
4. **Risks and Mitigation**
    - **Currency Volatility** (hedging strategies), **Regulatory Shifts** (compliance plan), **Competition** (product differentiation).
    - **Mitigation**: Hedging policy, local JV partnerships, robust R&D budget, optional M&A pipeline for bolt-ons.
5. **Exit Strategy**
    - **Preferred Options**: IPO, strategic sale, or secondary LBO. Possibly a **dividend recap** if the sponsor wants partial liquidity.
    - **Timeline**: Typically 5–7 years (adjust if you foresee a faster or slower path to value creation).
    - **Potential Buyers**: Large strategic players, international conglomerates, or another PE sponsor.

Memo Enhancement Tips

- Incorporate graphics (charts, bullet points) to highlight the most essential data (e.g., IRR over time, synergy breakdown).
- Use short “case vignettes” or anecdotal evidence (like a key competitor’s success story) to bolster your rationale.

Module 3: Investment Committee Presentation

Present your recommendations to a **simulated Investment Committee**. The goal is to **secure final approval**, demonstrating strategic, financial, and operational rigor.

Presentation Guidelines

1. **Structure and Content**
    - **Opening Slide**: Crisp 1-slide "deal snapshot": EV, leverage, IRR, key rationale.
    - **Financial Highlights**: Summarize IRR ranges, DSCR across scenarios, capital structure, synergy gains.
    - **Strategic Initiatives**: Outline the big plays—cost savings, market expansions, digital transformations, AI usage.
    - **Risk Analysis**: Highlight top 3–4 major risks (e.g., competitor moves, interest rate spikes, regulatory surprises) and your mitigation strategies (hedging, local partnerships, AI-based cost tracking, etc.).
2. **Delivery**
    - Be **concise** but ensure clarity of each point.
    - Deploy visuals (graphs, dashboards) to illustrate model findings—especially scenario outcomes.
    - Avoid jargon. Keep finance or operational terms accessible to a broad committee.
3. **Q&A Preparation**
    - Anticipate questions on **valuation assumptions**, synergy feasibility, and potential exit timing.
    - Provide **data-driven** answers. Reference your scenario analyses or external comps as needed.

Section	Key Content	Time Allocation
Deal Overview	Target summary, investment thesis	5 minutes
Financial Metrics	IRR, DSCR, scenario analysis, synergy valuation	10 minutes
Strategic Plan	Cost improvements, growth expansions, tech integrations	10 minutes
Risks & Mitigation	Top risks, proposed solutions, fallback plans	5 minutes
Q&A	Field committee questions	10 minutes

Presentation Enhancement Tips

- Consider role-playing: have one participant as the "CFO," another as "Head of Strategy," etc.
- Provide a short 1-page takeaway (handout) for quick reference during Q&A.

Optional Upgrades to Capstone Projects

To **personalize** and **deepen** your learning, consider weaving in one or more of these advanced elements:

1. **AI-Driven Insights**
    - Integrate AI-based revenue or cost projections (like demand forecasting or margin optimization).
    - Include AI-based red-flag detection during due diligence (identifying unusual liabilities or compliance issues).
    - Show how data analytics or machine learning improves synergy capture or supply chain optimization.
2. **ESG Metrics**
    - Align the deal strategy with **Environmental, Social, and Governance** goals (e.g., reducing carbon footprint, improving labor practices).
    - Explore **sustainability-linked financing** or **unitranche + green bond** combos that reward ESG progress.
    - Incorporate a "Green Audit" in post-acquisition operational checklists.
3. **Emerging Market Complexity**
    - Evaluate currency exposure and potential hedging solutions if dealing with multi-currency revenues or debt.
    - Factor in **political risk** or uncertain legal frameworks that might slow expansions.
    - Partner with local firms for easier regulatory navigation or brand trust.
4. **Secondary Themes**
    - **Dividend Recapitalization**: Model how you might extract cash after hitting certain performance milestones.
    - **Bolt-On M&A**: Explore adding a smaller acquisition to accelerate synergy or expand product lines.
    - **Management Equity Rollover**: Show how management invests or retains stake, aligning incentives.

Conclusion

The **Capstone Project** bridges theory and practice, giving you a real-world sense of **complete LBO execution**. By **modeling deals**, creating **compelling investment memos**, and presenting to a **simulated IC**, participants gain not just technical competence, but the **strategic perspective** and **presentation acumen** required in real-world private equity transactions.

Remember: This capstone is not just an exercise in numbers, but in **critical thinking**—pushing you to weigh **risks**, **strategic options**, and **execution feasibility**. The ultimate goal is to build confidence and expertise that will translate seamlessly to **live deal environments**.

Self-Study Questions

1. **What are the key components** of an effective LBO model (beyond the basics of revenue, cost, capital structure)?
2. **How can scenario analysis** dramatically enhance decision-making and risk management in leveraged deals?
3. **Which factors** should be emphasized most in an investment memo for an LBO—financials, operational strategy, or risk mitigation—and why?
4. **What tactics** can presenters use to effectively address challenges or tough questions during an investment committee Q&A?
5. **Discuss the roles** of AI and ESG metrics in enhancing modern LBOs. How might these factors influence valuation or financing terms?

Lesson Takeaways

- **Robust LBO Modeling**: Demands meticulous inputs, multi-scenario frameworks, and well-structured capital.
- **Investment Memo Excellence**: Balances **quantitative rigor** with **strategic clarity**—a must to persuade stakeholders.
- **Effective Communication**: Crisp, confident presentations are crucial to securing buy-in from sponsors or co-investors.
- **Advanced Tactics**: AI integration, ESG considerations, and emerging market complexities can boost both returns and resilience of the deal.

LBO Excellence and Upskilling

Case Study Playbook for LBO Analysis

Purpose of the Case Study Playbook

This playbook provides a step-by-step framework to systematically analyze leveraged buyout (LBO) case studies. It equips participants with templates, checklists, and methodologies to replicate real-world deal evaluations and sharpen their decision-making skills. By adopting a structured approach, participants can identify value creation opportunities, assess risks, and propose actionable strategies for successful LBO execution.

Step-by-Step Methodology for LBO Case Analysis

1. Understanding the Context

- **Objective:** Identify the key characteristics of the deal and define the analytical scope.
- **Steps:**
    1. Review the target's business model, industry, and historical performance.
    2. Identify the stakeholders involved (e.g., sponsors, management, lenders).
    3. Define the objectives of the case (e.g., feasibility assessment, optimization).

Key Question	Example Insight
What is the target company's core value proposition?	Dominates the regional retail market with a 35% market share.
What are the primary challenges in this deal?	Declining foot traffic and high fixed costs.

2. Financial Analysis and Valuation

- **Objective:** Quantify the target's financial health and determine a realistic valuation.
- **Steps:**
    1. Assess historical revenue, EBITDA, and margins.
    2. Calculate key metrics (e.g., EV/EBITDA, P/E ratios).
    3. Perform a discounted cash flow (DCF) valuation.
    4. Compare to precedent transactions and industry peers.

Metric	Formula	Purpose
EV/EBITDA		Assess operational performance valuation.
Debt Service Coverage Ratio (DSCR)		Ensure debt obligations are serviceable.
Internal Rate of Return (IRR)	Iterative calculation using cash flows	Determine annualized return on equity.

3. Strategic Assessment

- **Objective:** Identify operational and strategic opportunities for value creation.
- **Steps:**
    1. Evaluate revenue growth strategies (e.g., market expansion, product innovation).
    2. Analyze cost optimization opportunities (e.g., supply chain improvements, workforce restructuring).
    3. Assess the competitive landscape and market trends.

Strategic Lever	Example Initiative	Potential Outcome
Revenue Growth	Expand e-commerce channels	15% increase in total sales by Year 3.
Cost Optimization	Consolidate redundant facilities	Annual savings of $10M.
Digital Transformation	Implement AI-driven inventory management	Reduce inventory holding costs by 20%.

4. Risk Assessment and Mitigation

- **Objective:** Identify key risks and propose strategies to mitigate them.
- **Steps:**
    1. Evaluate financial risks (e.g., over-leverage, interest rate volatility).
    2. Assess operational risks (e.g., integration challenges, supply chain disruptions).
    3. Identify market risks (e.g., economic downturns, regulatory changes).

Risk Category	Specific Risk	Mitigation Strategy
Financial	Rising interest rates	Hedge interest rate exposure.
Operational	Delayed cost-savings realization	Phase implementation of cost reductions.
Market	Regulatory hurdles in new markets	Engage local advisory firms.

5. Structuring the Deal

- **Objective:** Optimize the capital structure to balance risk and return.
- **Steps:**
  1. Design the financing mix (e.g., senior debt, mezzanine debt, equity).
  2. Calculate key leverage metrics and ensure covenant compliance.
  3. Align financing terms with projected cash flows and repayment capacity.

Financing Layer	Characteristic	Proportion in Deal
Senior Debt	Secured by company assets; lowest interest	50%-70% of total financing.
Mezzanine Debt	Subordinated, higher interest, flexible terms	10%-20% of total financing.
Sponsor Equity	Equity investment by financial sponsor	20%-30% of total financing.

6. Exit Planning

- **Objective:** Define the optimal exit strategy to maximize returns.
- **Steps:**
    1. Evaluate exit options: IPO, strategic sale, secondary buyout.
    2. Align timing with market conditions and value creation milestones.
    3. Calculate projected equity returns and prepare exit scenarios.

Exit Option	Pros	Cons
IPO	High valuation potential	Market volatility risk.
Strategic Sale	Access to synergies for buyer	Requires extensive buyer negotiations.
Secondary Buyout	Quick execution	Lower valuation compared to IPO.

Templates and Tools

Case Study Evaluation Checklist

Section	Key Question
Target Overview	What is the target's core value proposition?
Financial Metrics	Does the target meet leverage and IRR goals?
Strategic Plan	Are value creation levers realistic?
Risks and Mitigation	Are major risks identified and addressed?
Exit Strategy	Is the exit plan aligned with market trends?

Sample Financial Metrics Table

Metric	Base Case	Downside Case	Upside Case
Revenue Growth (%)	5%	2%	8%
EBITDA Margin (%)	12%	10%	14%
IRR (%)	25%	15%	32%

Conclusion

The Case Study Playbook provides a robust framework for analyzing and executing LBO case studies. By leveraging structured methodologies, templates, and strategic insights, participants can develop a comprehensive understanding of deal evaluation and execution. This approach ensures systematic decision-making, risk mitigation, and optimal value creation in real-world scenarios.

LBO Value Creation Metrics

Purpose of the Value Creation Metrics Framework

Value creation is the cornerstone of leveraged buyouts (LBOs), transforming acquired companies into high-performing assets. This appendix introduces advanced Key Performance Indicators (KPIs) that measure success across operational, strategic, and financial dimensions during the ownership period. By leveraging these metrics, practitioners can track progress, identify challenges, and refine strategies to maximize returns.

Purpose of Value Creation Metrics

1. **Early Identification**
   Identify underperformance early in the process.
2. **Focus on Impact**
   Concentrate on crucial areas: operational efficiency, growth strategies, capital returns.
3. **Goal Alignment**
   Align performance with long-term financial objectives.

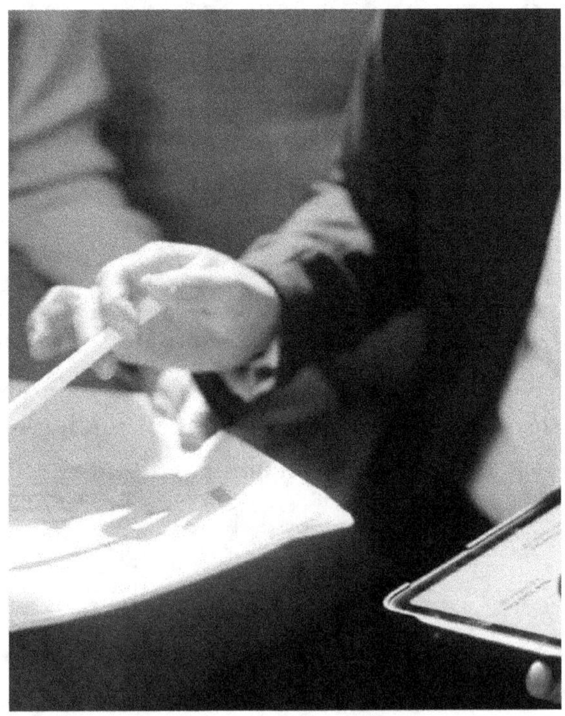

Categories of Value Creation Metrics

1. Operational KPIs

Operational KPIs focus on improving efficiency and profitability by enhancing core business processes and resource utilization.

Metric	Definition	Application	Example Goal
Revenue Per Employee	Revenue generated per employee	Measures workforce productivity	Increase by 10% through automation
Inventory Turnover		Assesses supply chain efficiency	Improve from 6x to 8x annually
Customer Retention Rate	Percentage of customers retained year-over-year	Tracks customer loyalty	Achieve 85% retention post-digital transformation
OPEX as % of Revenue	Ratio of operating expenses to revenue	Identifies cost optimization opportunities	Reduce from 30% to 25%

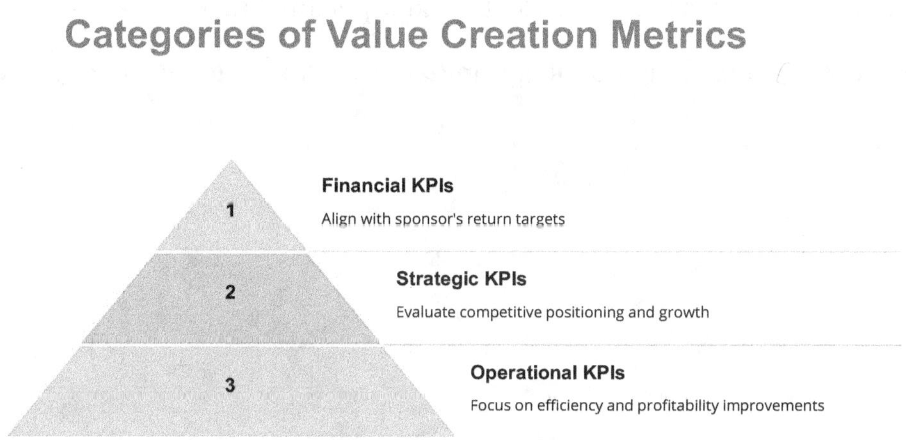

Advanced Techniques:

- **Process Mining:** Use AI-driven tools to identify bottlenecks in production or service delivery.
- **IoT Integration:** Leverage real-time data to optimize inventory and equipment utilization.

2. Strategic KPIs

Strategic KPIs evaluate progress in achieving long-term growth objectives and competitive positioning.

Metric	Definition	Application	Example Goal
Market Share Growth	Change in the company's market share	Reflects competitive performance	Increase market share by 5%
R&D Effectiveness		Tracks ROI on innovation efforts	Generate $50M in new product revenue
Digital Revenue Mix	% of revenue from digital channels	Monitors digital transformation progress	Reach 40% digital sales contribution
Expansion Success Rate	% of successful new market entries	Evaluates execution of geographic growth	Achieve 80% success in market launches

Advanced Techniques:

- **Geo-Analytics:** Use location-based data to identify high-potential markets.
- **Customer Journey Mapping:** Align strategic initiatives with customer touchpoints to boost engagement.

Operational KPIs Overview

Revenue Per Employee

Tracks productivity, aiming for growth through automation.

Inventory Turnover

Monitors supply chain efficiency to minimize holding costs.

Customer Retention Rate

Ensures loyalty during transformations like digital shifts.

OPEX as % of Revenue

Highlights cost optimization opportunities.

3. Financial KPIs

Financial KPIs measure the profitability, liquidity, and capital efficiency of the portfolio company, ensuring alignment with the sponsor's return targets.

Metric	Definition	Application	Example Goal
ROIC (Return on Invested Capital)		Evaluates overall capital efficiency	Improve from 12% to 15%
Leverage Ratio		Monitors debt levels relative to earnings	Reduce from 4.5x to 3.5x
Free Cash Flow Yield		Measures cash flow generation relative to valuation	Maintain 8% annually
Exit Multiple	Exit EV/EBITDA relative to entry multiple	Quantifies valuation improvement	Expand multiple from 8x to 10x

Advanced Techniques:

- **Scenario-Based Projections:** Model financial outcomes under various macroeconomic conditions.

- **Dynamic Cost Analysis:** Use predictive analytics to forecast expense trends and adjust in real-time.

Financial KPIs Overview

ROIC

Tracks returns, aiming to improve from 12% to 15%.

Leverage Ratio

Monitors debt, targeting a reduction from 4.5x to 3.5x EBITDA.

Free Cash Flow Yield

Measures cash flow relative to valuation, targeting 8% annually.

Exit Multiple

Quantifies valuation improvements, aiming to grow from 8x to 10x EBITDA.

Tracking and Reporting Framework

1. Real-Time Dashboards

- **Description:** Create dashboards to aggregate and visualize KPIs in real time.
- **Key Tools:** Tableau, Power BI, and custom Excel models.
- **Example:** A dashboard tracking EBITDA margin improvements, inventory turnover, and digital revenue growth in a single view.

2. Quarterly Reviews

- **Description:** Conduct comprehensive reviews of KPI performance against goals.
- **Purpose:** Identify variances and realign strategies to address shortfalls.

Template:

Metric	Target	Actual	Variance	Action Plan
Revenue Growth (%)	5%	4.2%	-0.8%	Enhance marketing spend in core markets
EBITDA Margin (%)	12%	11.5%	-0.5%	Streamline administrative costs
Market Share (%)	20%	21%	+1%	Focus on maintaining competitive edge

Linking Metrics to Value Creation Stages

Stage 1: Acquisition and Integration

- **Focus:** Establish baseline metrics and integrate operational systems.
- **Key Metrics:**
  - Baseline EBITDA Margin.
  - Employee Attrition Rate.
  - Cost-to-Revenue Ratio.

Stage 2: Operational Scaling

- **Focus:** Execute value creation initiatives to improve efficiency and profitability.
- **Key Metrics:**
  - Revenue Per Employee.
  - Inventory Turnover.
  - OPEX as % of Revenue.

Stage 3: Exit Preparation

- **Focus:** Maximize valuation through strategic positioning and financial optimization.
- **Key Metrics:**
  - ROIC.
  - Exit Multiple.
  - Free Cash Flow Yield.

Advanced Reporting: The Balanced LBO Scorecard

Integrate KPIs across operational, strategic, and financial dimensions into a balanced scorecard.

Dimension	Metric	Target	Actual	Variance
Operational	Revenue Per Employee	$250,000	$240,000	-$10,000
	Inventory Turnover	8x	7.5x	-0.5x
Strategic	Market Share Growth (%)	5%	4.8%	-0.2%
	Digital Revenue Mix (%)	40%	38%	-2%
Financial	ROIC (%)	15%	14%	-1%
	Exit Multiple	10x	9.5x	-0.5x

Conclusion

Advanced KPIs for LBO value creation provide a holistic framework to measure progress and outcomes during the ownership period. By combining operational, strategic, and financial metrics with cutting-edge tools and reporting techniques, private equity sponsors can ensure a data-driven approach to value creation. This not only maximizes returns but also builds a transparent and adaptable roadmap for long-term success.

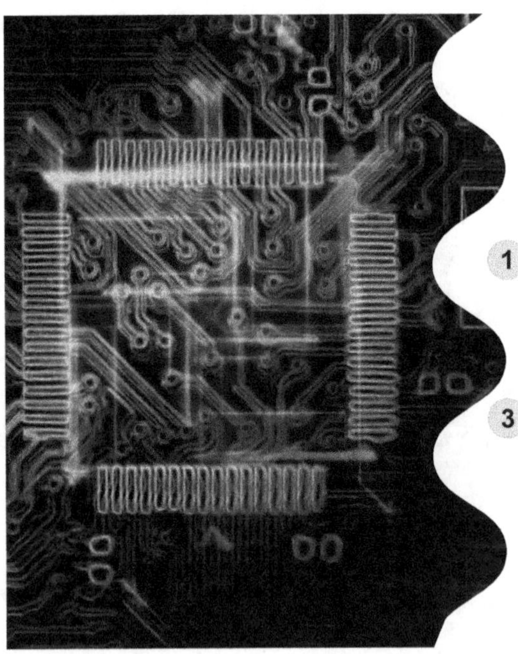

Advanced Reporting Techniques

1. **Real-Time Dashboards**
   Platforms like Tableau and Power BI aggregate and visualize metrics.
2. **Quarterly Reviews**
   Detailed reviews compare target metrics to actuals, creating action plans.
3. **Predictive Analytics**
   Machine learning models forecast future performance and identify potential risks.
4. **Integrated Reporting Systems**
   Comprehensive platforms connect financial, operational, and strategic data for holistic insights.

Comparative Analysis of Financing Structures in LBOs

Purpose of the Comparative Analysis

Choosing the right financing structure is a critical element of executing a successful leveraged buyout (LBO). This appendix provides an in-depth comparison of key financing options, including unitranche, mezzanine, and high-yield bonds. It highlights the pros, cons, and best-use scenarios for each, enabling participants to align financing strategies with deal objectives.

Overview of Financing Structures

Financing Option	Definition	Key Characteristics
Unitranche Debt	A single-layer debt combining senior and subordinated debt	Blended interest rate; simpler structure
Mezzanine Debt	Subordinated debt with higher interest rates and flexible terms	Includes equity kickers in some cases
High-Yield Bonds	Unsecured, high-interest debt with fewer covenants	Commonly used for large-scale transactions

Detailed Comparison

1. Unitranche Debt

Aspect	Details
Definition	Combines senior and subordinated debt into a single tranche.
Interest Rate	Blended rate, slightly higher than senior debt but lower than mezzanine debt.
Structure	Single contract simplifies administration.
Best-Use Scenarios	Mid-market deals requiring flexibility and quick execution.

Pros:

- Simplifies debt structure with a single lender.
- Streamlines negotiations and reduces administrative costs.
- Offers flexibility in repayment schedules.

Cons:

- Higher interest rates compared to traditional senior debt.
- Limited syndication options, potentially reducing access to large pools of capital.

Example Use Case:

- A $200M acquisition of a mid-sized logistics company requiring a streamlined financing approach to close the deal within tight deadlines.

2. Mezzanine Debt

Aspect	Details
Definition	Subordinated debt that bridges the gap between senior debt and equity.
Interest Rate	10%-15% on average, reflecting higher risk.
Structure	Includes payment-in-kind (PIK) interest or equity warrants in some cases.
Best-Use Scenarios	Deals with high growth potential or limited collateral.

Pros:

- Increases leverage capacity without diluting equity.
- Flexible repayment terms, often with deferred interest options.
- Aligns lender incentives with company performance through equity kickers.

Cons:

- Higher interest rates increase cost of capital.
- Subordinated position in capital structure means greater risk for lenders.

Example Use Case:

- Financing a $500M technology firm acquisition where future growth is expected to drive substantial equity returns.

3. High-Yield Bonds

Aspect	Details
Definition	Unsecured debt issued to institutional investors, offering high interest rates.
Interest Rate	Typically 7%-10%, higher than senior debt but lower than mezzanine.
Structure	Limited covenants, providing operational flexibility.
Best-Use Scenarios	Large-scale transactions where flexibility and quick capital access are priorities.

Pros:

- Less restrictive covenants compared to traditional loans.
- Attracts large pools of capital for significant financing needs.
- Long-term maturity allows for strategic use of cash flows.

Cons:

- Higher risk due to unsecured nature.
- Volatility in bond markets can impact pricing and availability.

Example Use Case:

- A $1.5B buyout of a global manufacturing company requiring substantial leverage with operational flexibility.

Decision-Making Framework

Key Questions to Determine Optimal Financing Structure:

Question	Consideration
What is the size of the transaction?	Large deals may require high-yield bonds for scalability.
How critical is speed to close?	Unitranche debt offers faster execution.
What is the company's growth potential?	High-growth companies benefit from mezzanine financing.
How much flexibility is needed?	High-yield bonds provide operational leeway.

Advanced Metrics for Evaluating Financing Structures

Metric	Formula	Purpose
Debt-to-Equity Ratio		Evaluates leverage in the capital structure.
Weighted Average Cost of Capital (WACC)		Determines overall cost of capital.
Interest Coverage Ratio		Assesses ability to service debt.

Tracking and Reporting Framework

Real-Time Financing Dashboard

- **Description:** Monitor debt performance metrics and compliance with covenants.
- **Key Tools:** Tableau, Power BI, Excel-integrated APIs.

Metric	Target	Actual	Variance
Interest Coverage Ratio	3.0x	2.8x	-0.2x
Leverage Ratio	4.0x	4.2x	+0.2x
Weighted Average Cost of Capital	8%	8.5%	+0.5%

Quarterly Financing Reviews

- **Purpose:** Evaluate the effectiveness of chosen financing structures and adjust strategies as needed.
- **Template:**

Aspect	Observation	Action Plan
Covenant Compliance	Minor breach in leverage covenant	Renegotiate terms with lenders.
Refinancing Opportunities	Declining interest rates	Explore refinancing senior debt.
Performance Metrics	Slight underperformance in DSCR	Enhance cash flow management.

Conclusion

A comparative understanding of financing structures is essential for tailoring LBO strategies to specific deal dynamics. By analyzing the trade-offs and scenarios for unitranche debt, mezzanine debt, and high-yield bonds, practitioners can make informed decisions that balance risk, flexibility, and return objectives. Advanced metrics and reporting tools further support effective execution and monitoring of financing strategies.

Innovative Exit Strategies in LBOs

Purpose of Innovative Exit Strategies

Traditional exit strategies such as IPOs, strategic sales, and secondary buyouts have dominated the private equity landscape. However, evolving market dynamics and stakeholder priorities have driven the emergence of innovative exit options, including SPAC mergers, employee ownership transitions, and hybrid models. This section explores these strategies, their applications, and comparative advantages to equip practitioners with creative tools for achieving optimal exits.

Categories of Exit Strategies

Traditional IPO
High-growth, robust branding.

Strategic Sale
Mature companies with synergy opportunities.

Secondary Buyout
Assets with remaining growth potential.

SPAC Merger
Accelerated access to public markets.

Employee Ownership Transition
Cultural preservation and retention.

Dual-Track Process
IPO and sale prepared simultaneously.

Categories of Exit Strategies

Exit Type	Description	Best-Use Scenario
Traditional IPO	Offering shares to the public via stock exchanges	High-growth companies with robust branding
Strategic Sale	Selling to an industry player for synergies	Mature companies with strategic appeal
Secondary Buyout	Selling to another private equity firm	Assets with remaining growth potential
SPAC Merger	Partnering with a Special Purpose Acquisition Company (SPAC)	Fast access to public markets
Employee Ownership Transition	Transferring ownership to employees via ESOPs	Stable companies with strong employee engagement
Dual-Track Process	Preparing for both IPO and sale simultaneously	Maximizes flexibility and competitive tension

Decision-Making Framework for Exit Strategies

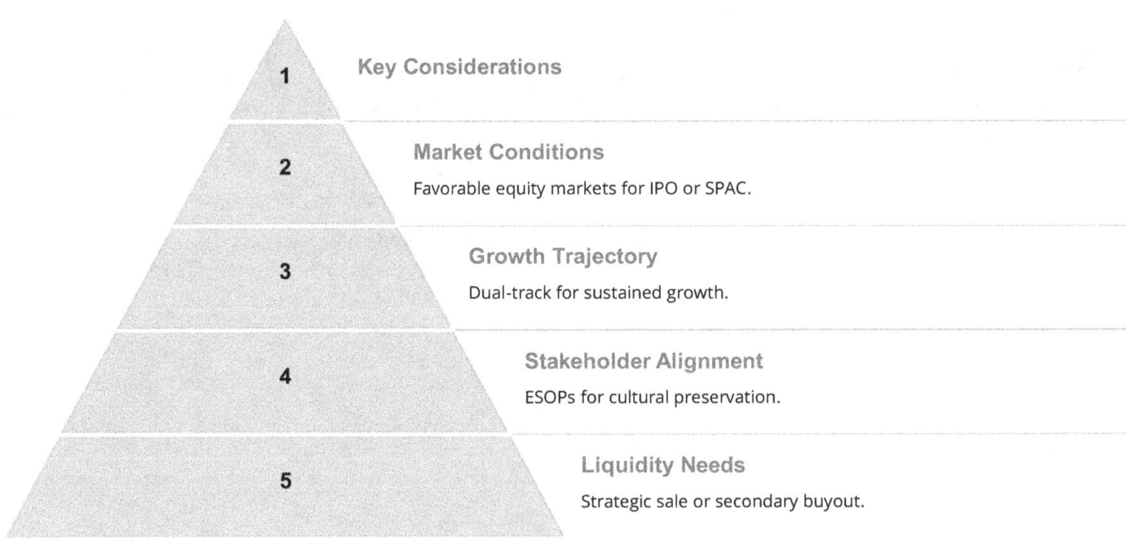

1. SPAC Mergers

Definition: A Special Purpose Acquisition Company (SPAC) is a publicly listed entity created to acquire private companies. In a SPAC merger, the target company goes public by merging with the SPAC.

Key Features:

- Faster access to public markets compared to a traditional IPO.
- Allows private equity sponsors to negotiate terms directly with SPAC managers.
- Provides upfront capital for the target's growth initiatives.

Pros	Cons
Accelerated time to market	Dilution of equity for existing stakeholders
Greater valuation predictability	Public perception risks due to SPAC performance
Access to experienced management	Regulatory scrutiny and evolving compliance standards

Example Scenario:

- A high-growth fintech company requiring immediate capital infusion for geographic expansion merges with a SPAC, achieving a $3 billion valuation within six months.

2. Employee Ownership Transitions

Definition: Employee Stock Ownership Plans (ESOPs) involve transferring ownership to employees, creating an incentive for long-term growth and retention.

Key Features:

- Aligns employee interests with organizational success.
- Offers tax benefits for sellers and the company.
- Preserves company culture during the ownership transition.

Pros	Cons
Retains institutional knowledge	Requires significant liquidity for initial funding
Enhances employee engagement	Complex valuation and administration
Tax-advantaged for sellers	Limited scalability for high-growth firms

Example Scenario:

- A family-owned logistics company transitions ownership to employees via an ESOP, ensuring business continuity while achieving a 25% equity stake exit for private equity sponsors.

3. Dual-Track Process

Definition: A dual-track process prepares a company for both an IPO and a strategic sale, allowing flexibility to pursue the most favorable outcome.

Key Features:

- Enhances competitive tension between potential buyers and public markets.
- Provides a fallback option if one track underperforms.
- Encourages thorough preparation of financials and governance.

Pros	Cons
Maximizes optionality	Higher costs due to dual preparation
Attracts multiple buyer types	Requires significant management bandwidth
Increases valuation pressure	Can extend the timeline for exit

Example Scenario:

- A SaaS company with strong recurring revenues initiates an IPO process while engaging in parallel discussions with strategic acquirers, ultimately opting for a $1.2 billion sale to a tech giant.

4. Hybrid Exits

Definition: Hybrid exits combine elements of multiple strategies, such as selling a minority stake to a strategic partner while retaining private equity ownership for future growth.

Key Features:

- Balances immediate liquidity with long-term value capture.
- Enables private equity sponsors to capitalize on upside potential.
- Reduces concentration risk for both buyers and sellers.

Pros	Cons
Flexible capital structuring	May complicate governance dynamics
Retains alignment of incentives	Requires robust agreements to manage conflicts
Allows gradual transition	Limited to specific scenarios

Example Scenario:

- A consumer goods company sells a 30% equity stake to a global retailer for strategic synergies while retaining the remainder for a future IPO.

Decision-Making Framework for Exit Strategies

Key Considerations:

Factor	Relevant Strategy	Consideration
Market Conditions	IPO, SPAC Merger	Favorable equity market performance
Growth Trajectory	Dual-Track Process, Hybrid Exit	Sustained revenue and profitability growth
Stakeholder Alignment	Employee Ownership Transition	Focus on long-term cultural preservation
Liquidity Needs	Strategic Sale, Secondary Buyout	Immediate capital requirements

Advanced Metrics for Evaluating Exit Options:

Metric	Definition	Purpose
Exit Multiple	Exit EV/EBITDA compared to entry multiple	Quantifies valuation improvement
Stakeholder Return	Total cash-on-cash return across equity holders	Measures equity realization success
Post-Exit Synergies	Estimated value from buyer synergies	Assesses strategic sale attractiveness

Tracking and Reporting Exit Outcomes

Post-Exit Analysis Dashboard

- **Description:** Track realized outcomes against initial targets.
- **Key Tools:** Tableau, Excel-based models, CRM integration.

Metric	Target	Actual	Variance
Exit Valuation ($M)	1,000	950	-50
Cash-on-Cash Return (x)	3.0x	2.8x	-0.2x
Time to Exit (Months)	24	28	+4

Tracking and Reporting Exit Outcomes

1 **Post-Exit Analysis Dashboard**

Metrics: Valuation, cash-on-cash return, exit timeline.

2 **Example Reporting Framework**

Target vs. Actual: Valuation: $1B target, $950M achieved (-$50M variance). Cash-on-Cash Return: 3.0x target, 2.8x achieved.

3 **Tools**

Tableau, Excel models.

Conclusion

Innovative exit strategies expand the toolkit for private equity sponsors, enabling them to align exits with evolving market conditions and stakeholder priorities. By considering SPAC mergers, employee ownership transitions, dual-track processes, and hybrid models, practitioners can maximize returns and flexibility while mitigating risks. This strategic approach ensures adaptability and success in an ever-changing investment landscape.

Crisis Management in LBOs

Purpose of Crisis Management in LBOs

Leveraged buyouts (LBOs) are inherently risky, relying on high leverage to achieve amplified returns. Economic downturns, market disruptions, and unexpected operational challenges can magnify these risks, jeopardizing value creation and solvency. This section provides a comprehensive framework for navigating crises, equipping sponsors and management teams with strategies to preserve resilience and adapt effectively.

Challenges Faced in LBO Crises

Liquidity Constraints	Limited cash flow increases default risk
Revenue Declines	Demand drops reduce EBITDA and valuations
Supply Chain Disruptions	Delays and interruptions increase costs
Regulatory Shocks	Rapid policy changes elevate compliance burdens

Key Challenges During Crises

Challenge	Description	Impact on LBOs
Liquidity Constraints	Limited cash flow to service debt	Increased risk of default
Revenue Declines	Sudden drops in demand or sales	Reduced EBITDA and valuation
Supply Chain Disruptions	Interruptions in production or logistics	Higher costs, delayed operations
Regulatory Shocks	Rapid policy changes affecting operations	Increased compliance costs

Strategies to Preserve Liquidity

1 **Debt Restructuring**

Negotiate covenant relief and extend maturities. Example: Transition to interest-only payments.

2 **Working Capital Optimization**

Accelerate receivables collection. Example: Generate $10M through early payments and extended supplier cycles.

3 **Contingency Financing**

Tap revolving credit facilities. Example: Secure $15M from asset sales for immediate liquidity.

1. Building a Crisis Management Framework

Key Components:

1. **Early Warning Systems:**
    - Monitor macroeconomic indicators, customer trends, and industry-specific risks.
    - Example: Implement dashboards tracking debt coverage ratios, inventory levels, and market conditions.

Metric	Purpose	Action Trigger
Debt Service Coverage Ratio (DSCR)	Assess ability to meet debt obligations	DSCR < 1.5 triggers cash flow review
Working Capital Turnover	Evaluate liquidity and operational efficiency	Sudden drops signal potential constraints
Customer Retention Rate	Track stability of revenue base	Retention below 80% prompts intervention

2. **Scenario Planning:**
    - Develop base, downside, and upside cases to stress-test financial models.
    - Incorporate variables such as revenue declines, interest rate hikes, and operational disruptions.

Scenario	Revenue Decline	Cost Increase	IRR Impact
Base Case	5%	2%	20%
Downside Case	15%	5%	12%
Upside Case	-2% (growth)	0%	28%

2. Liquidity Management During Crises

Strategies to Preserve Liquidity:

1. **Debt Restructuring:**
    - Negotiate with lenders for covenant relief or payment deferrals.
    - Example: Extend maturities or transition to interest-only periods to alleviate cash flow pressure.
2. **Working Capital Optimization:**
    - Accelerate receivables collection and renegotiate supplier terms.
    - Example: Offer early payment discounts to customers while securing longer payment cycles from suppliers.

Action	Expected Outcome
Renegotiate payment terms	Free up $10M in short-term cash
Sell non-core assets	Generate $15M for immediate liquidity

3. **Contingency Financing:**
    - Secure lines of credit or bridge financing for unexpected needs.
    - Example: Tap revolving credit facilities to cover urgent operational costs.

3. Operational Resilience Strategies

Key Focus Areas:

1. **Cost Control:**
   - Identify and eliminate non-essential expenses without impairing core operations.
   - Example: Freeze hiring, renegotiate leases, and consolidate facilities.
2. **Supply Chain Stabilization:**
   - Diversify suppliers and stock critical inventory to avoid disruptions.
   - Example: Shift from single-source suppliers to regional alternatives.

Tactic	Benefit	Example
Centralize Procurement	Achieve economies of scale	Save 10% on bulk purchases
Invest in Automation	Reduce dependency on manual processes	Cut labor costs by $2M annually

Strengthening Operational Resilience

Cost Control

Freeze hiring, renegotiate leases. Save $2M annually by consolidating offices.

Supply Chain Stabilization

Diversify suppliers and stock critical inventory. Shift to regional suppliers for risk mitigation.

Process Optimization

Implement centralized procurement and automation to increase efficiency.

4. Communication and Stakeholder Management

Best Practices:

1. **Transparent Communication:**
    - Keep lenders, investors, and employees informed about challenges and mitigation strategies.
    - Example: Share monthly updates on financial performance and operational adjustments.
2. **Stakeholder Alignment:**
    - Foster collaboration among sponsors, management, and lenders to align crisis priorities.
    - Example: Host weekly calls with lenders to renegotiate covenants based on real-time updates.

Stakeholder	Communication Objective	Action Plan
Lenders	Build trust, request flexibility	Propose covenant-light restructuring
Employees	Maintain morale during cost cuts	Offer transparent rationale and timelines
Customers	Assure service continuity	Deploy proactive outreach campaigns

Engaging Stakeholders During Crises

Transparent Communication

Share monthly updates with lenders, investors, and employees.

Stakeholder Alignment

Host weekly calls to foster collaboration and renegotiate terms.

Targeted Engagement

Tailor communication for each stakeholder group (e.g., lenders: covenant restructuring; employees: morale building).

5. Leveraging Technology in Crisis Management

Digital Tools:

1. **Predictive Analytics:**
    - Use AI to forecast revenue drops or supply chain risks.
    - Example: Predictive models identify a 20% revenue decline three months in advance, allowing pre-emptive cost reductions.
2. **Real-Time Dashboards:**
    - Aggregate data across financial, operational, and market metrics to facilitate decision-making.
    - Example: Monitor liquidity and debt service capacity in real-time using Power BI.
3. **Automation:**
    - Streamline repetitive tasks to reduce costs and enhance efficiency.
    - Example: Automate payroll processing to save $500K annually during cash-strapped periods.

Tool	Application	Outcome
Tableau	Real-time KPI visualization	Faster crisis response
SAP Ariba	Supplier management and cost tracking	Improved procurement efficiency
UiPath	Process automation	Reduced manual errors and time savings

6. Post-Crisis Recovery and Value Rebuilding

Key Recovery Strategies – a combo:

1. **Operational Realignment:**
    - Prioritize investments in high-growth areas identified during the crisis.
    - Example: Expand digital sales channels after stabilizing operations.
2. **Debt Optimization:**
    - Refinance debt to lock in favorable terms during recovery periods.
    - Example: Replace high-interest mezzanine debt with lower-cost senior debt.
3. **Rebuilding Employee Morale:**
    - Recognize and reward teams for navigating the crisis successfully.
    - Example: Offer equity incentives to retain top talent post-crisis.

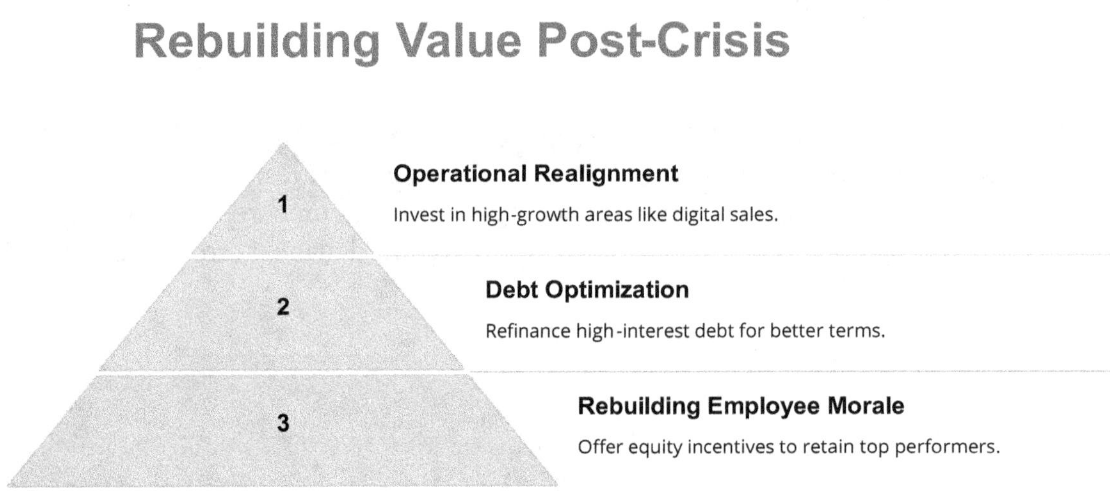

Crisis Management Checklist

Category	Key Question	Action Plan
Early Warning Systems	Are critical metrics monitored regularly?	Implement real-time dashboards
Liquidity	Are contingency plans in place?	Secure revolving credit facilities
Stakeholder Management	Are communication protocols clear?	Schedule bi-weekly updates with lenders
Recovery	Is the post-crisis strategy defined?	Focus on high-growth opportunities

Comprehensive Crisis Management Checklist

Category	Question	Action
Early Warning Systems	Are critical metrics monitored?	Implement real-time dashboards
Liquidity	Are contingency plans in place?	Secure credit facilities
Stakeholder Management	Are communication protocols clear?	Schedule bi-weekly lender updates
Recovery	Is the post-crisis strategy defined?	Focus on growth opportunities

Conclusion

Crisis management is an essential skill in LBO execution, ensuring resilience and value preservation during volatile periods. By implementing early warning systems, optimizing liquidity, and leveraging technology, sponsors can navigate disruptions effectively. Clear communication and a focus on recovery strategies further strengthen the pathway to long-term success.

Psychological Aspects of Deal-Making in LBOs

Purpose of Addressing Psychological Aspects

Leveraged buyouts (LBOs) are not solely defined by financial metrics and strategic execution—they are also influenced by human dynamics. Behavioral economics, negotiation psychology, and team interactions play a critical role in decision-making, stakeholder alignment, and deal outcomes. This section explores these psychological factors and provides actionable insights to integrate the human element into LBO processes effectively.

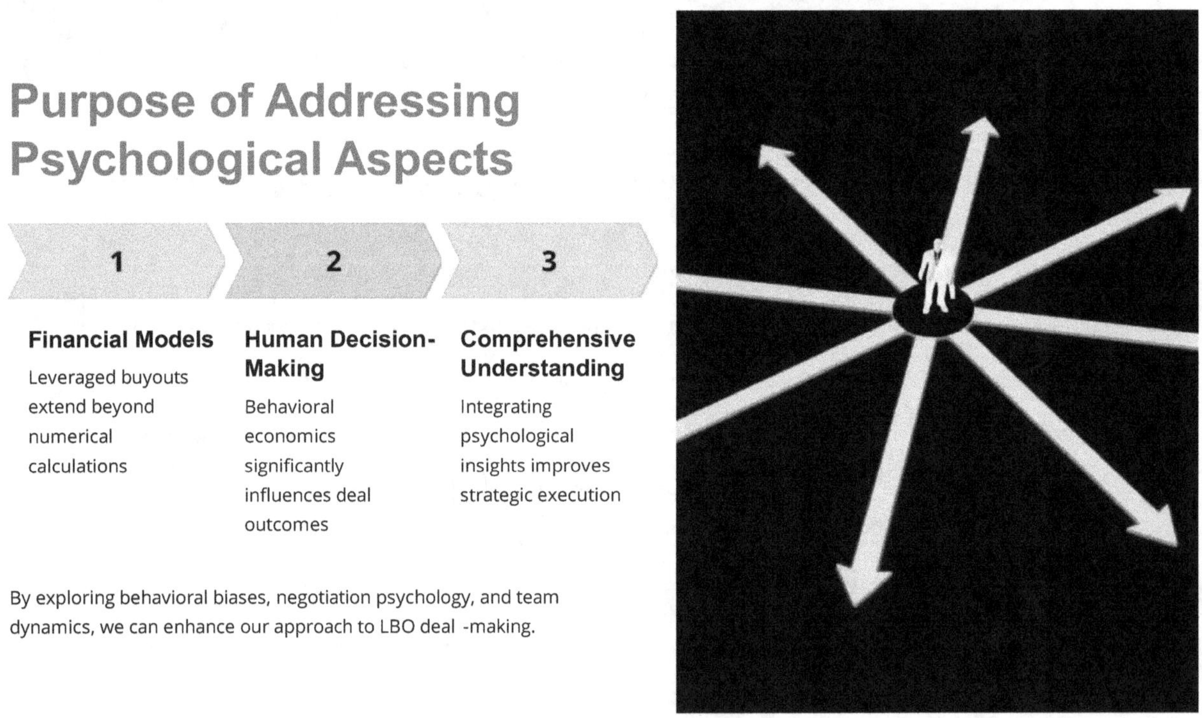

Core Psychological Elements in LBO Deal-Making

Psychological Aspect	Definition	Application in LBOs
Behavioral Biases	Cognitive shortcuts that influence decision-making	Avoiding overconfidence or anchoring during valuation
Negotiation Psychology	Techniques to influence outcomes through strategic interactions	Enhances stakeholder alignment and deal terms
Team Dynamics	Interpersonal relationships within and across teams	Ensures cohesive execution across stakeholders

Core Psychological Elements in LBO Deal-Making

Behavioral Biases

Cognitive shortcuts that can lead to errors in judgment.

Negotiation Psychology

Understanding the dynamics of negotiation and using strategies to influence outcomes.

Team Dynamics

Importance of collaboration and communication across teams.

1. Behavioral Biases in LBO Decision-Making

Key Biases and Their Impact:

Bias	Definition	Impact on LBOs
Anchoring Bias	Relying too heavily on initial information	Inflates valuations based on seller's opening offer
Overconfidence Bias	Overestimating one's ability to predict outcomes	Leads to aggressive projections and leverage
Confirmation Bias	Seeking information that supports existing beliefs	Skews due diligence and risk assessments

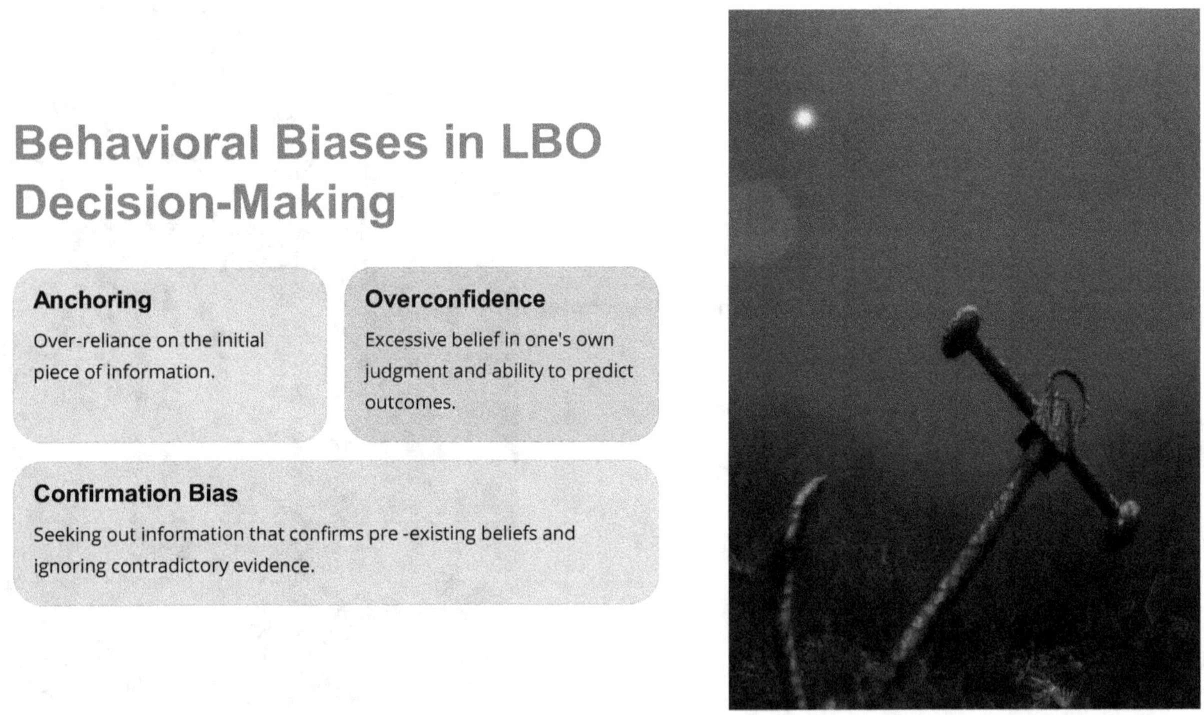

Mitigation Strategies:

1. **Anchoring Bias:** Conduct independent valuations before engaging with sellers.
2. **Overconfidence Bias:** Stress-test models with conservative downside scenarios.
3. **Confirmation Bias:** Assign a devil's advocate role during due diligence.

Example Scenario:

- **Context:** A PE sponsor accepts the seller's proposed valuation without thorough independent analysis.
- **Outcome:** Post-acquisition financial metrics underperform due to overestimated synergies.
- **Solution:** Implement cross-team reviews to challenge assumptions early.

Negotiation Psychology in LBO Transactions

1. **Framing**
   Presenting information in a way that influences perceptions.
2. **Reciprocity**
   The tendency to respond to actions with similar actions.
3. **BATNA**
   Best Alternative To a Negotiated Agreement.

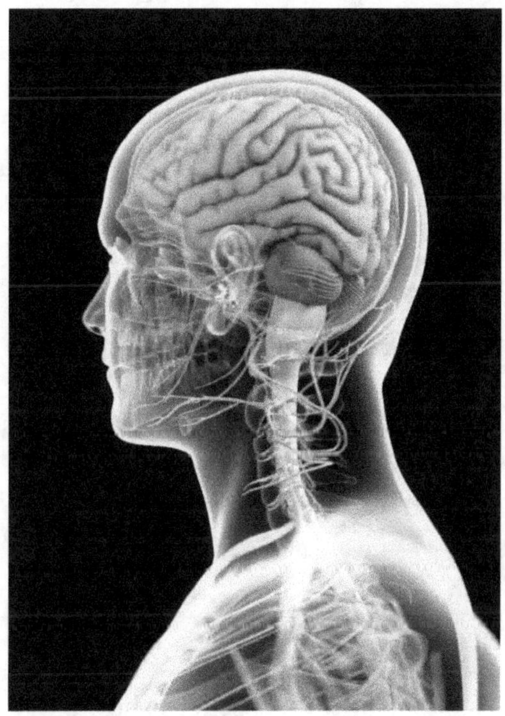

2. Negotiation Psychology in LBO Transactions

Negotiation is a high-stakes psychological interplay, requiring understanding of both financial objectives and human behavior.

Key Principles:

1. **Framing:**
    - Present terms in a way that highlights mutual benefits.
    - Example: Emphasize long-term synergies rather than short-term price adjustments.
2. **Reciprocity:**
    - Small concessions encourage counterparties to reciprocate.
    - Example: Agreeing to flexible payment terms can help secure seller warranties.
3. **BATNA (Best Alternative to a Negotiated Agreement):**
    - Clearly define alternatives to strengthen leverage.
    - Example: Prepare alternative financing sources to counter lender demands.

Tactic	Psychological Basis	Application
Anchoring Opening Offers	Leverages the anchoring effect	Propose aggressive initial terms to set the tone
Mirroring	Builds rapport by reflecting counterpart's behavior	Enhances trust and collaboration
Strategic Silence	Creates discomfort, prompting counterpart to fill gaps	Encourages revealing of hidden priorities

Example Scenario:

- **Context:** A seller is hesitant to include a MAC (Material Adverse Change) clause.
- **Action:** Buyer offers flexibility on working capital targets in exchange for the clause.
- **Outcome:** Deal terms are aligned without compromising core protections.

3. Team Dynamics in LBO Execution

Importance of Cohesive Teams:

Dynamic	Description	Impact
Internal Alignment	Clear communication and role clarity within the sponsor team	Ensures efficient execution of deal strategies
Cross-Stakeholder Collaboration	Alignment between PE firms, lenders, and management	Facilitates smoother negotiations and implementation
Conflict Resolution	Mechanisms to address disputes effectively	Minimizes delays and miscommunication

Strategies for Effective Team Dynamics:

1. **Pre-Deal Alignment:**
    - Define objectives, key metrics, and individual responsibilities before engaging with external stakeholders.
2. **Stakeholder Mapping:**
    - Identify key decision-makers and their priorities across sellers, lenders, and advisors.
3. **Regular Check-Ins:**
    - Establish weekly updates to align on progress and address emerging issues.

Example Scenario:

- **Issue:** Internal disagreements over the proposed financing structure delay negotiations.
- **Solution:** Host a workshop to align the investment team's priorities and finalize terms collaboratively.

Tools and Frameworks

Behavioral Decision-Making Checklist:

Question	Purpose	Action Required
Are valuations free from anchoring bias?	Ensures accurate pricing	Conduct independent financial analysis
Have risks been adequately challenged?	Mitigates overconfidence in projections	Assign a devil's advocate during due diligence
Are team dynamics supporting execution?	Promotes efficiency	Conduct post-mortem reviews post-negotiation

Negotiation Success Scorecard:

Dimension	Metric	Target
Stakeholder Alignment	% of aligned negotiation terms	90%+ agreement
Concessions Effectiveness	Ratio of gains to concessions	>2:1
Closing Time	Time to finalize deal post-term sheet	<60 days

Conclusion

The psychological aspects of LBO deal-making provide a critical lens through which to evaluate and execute transactions. By understanding behavioral biases, mastering negotiation tactics, and fostering strong team dynamics, private equity sponsors can navigate complex deals with precision and confidence. Integrating these human factors into traditional financial frameworks ensures a holistic approach to maximizing value in LBOs.

Negotiation Strategies in LBOs

Purpose of Negotiation Strategies in LBOs

Negotiation is a critical skill in the execution of leveraged buyouts (LBOs). This section provides insights into negotiating key terms such as purchase agreements, representations and warranties, and debt covenants. By mastering these tactics, participants can secure favorable deal terms, mitigate risks, and align stakeholder interests for long-term success.

Why Negotiation is Critical in LBOs

Amplified Risk and Opportunity

Balance between risk and return in high-leverage transactions

Stakeholder Alignment

Foster consensus between buyers, sellers, and lenders

Comprehensive Approach

Cover financial, operational, and legal dimensions

Key Negotiation Areas in LBOs

Negotiation Area	Description	Significance
Purchase Agreements	Establish terms of sale, including price and conditions	Defines the financial and legal framework for the deal
Representations and Warranties	Ensures the seller's accountability for undisclosed risks	Protects the buyer from future liabilities
Debt Covenants	Specifies restrictions on borrower activities	Safeguards lender interests while maintaining flexibility

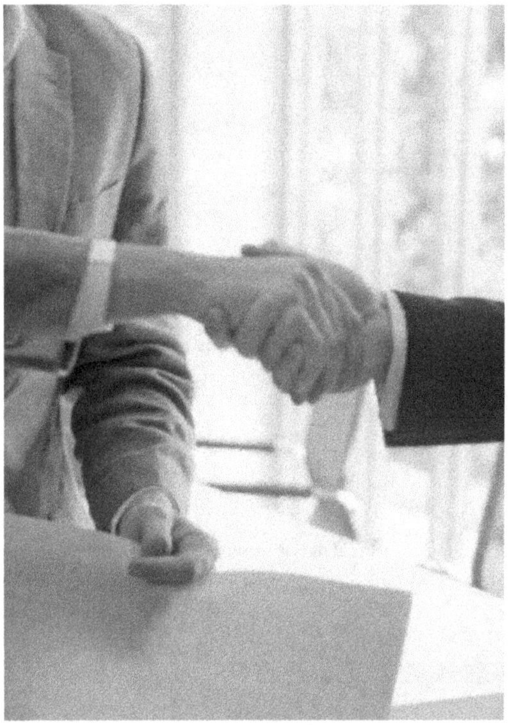

Crafting Favorable Purchase Agreements

1. **Purchase Price Adjustments**
   Reflect changes in working capital, use earn-outs
2. **Closing Conditions**
   Address approvals, contingencies, MAC clauses
3. **Tactics**
   Model thresholds, clear earn-outs, symmetrical MAC clauses

1. Negotiating Purchase Agreements

Key Components:

1. **Purchase Price Adjustments:**
    - **Goal:** Align the purchase price with accurate valuations at closing.
    - **Mechanisms:**
        - Working Capital Adjustments: Reflect changes in net working capital between signing and closing.
        - Earn-Outs: Link part of the purchase price to post-acquisition performance.

Mechanism	Definition	Negotiation Focus
Working Capital Adjustment	Adjust purchase price based on final working capital	Agree on targets and thresholds
Earn-Out	Contingent payments tied to future performance	Define metrics and payment timelines

2. **Closing Conditions:**
    - Includes regulatory approvals, financing contingencies, and material adverse change (MAC) clauses.

Negotiation Tactics:

- Use detailed financial models to set realistic working capital targets.
- Propose symmetrical MAC clauses to balance risk between buyer and seller.
- Establish clear timelines for earn-outs to avoid disputes.

Example Scenario:

- **Context:** Buyer discovers declining working capital during due diligence.
- **Resolution:** Negotiate a $5M reduction in the purchase price via working capital adjustments.

2. Representations and Warranties

Key Components:

1. **Seller Representations:**
   - Statements about the target company's financials, operations, and legal compliance.
2. **Warranties:**
   - Commitments to indemnify the buyer for inaccuracies or undisclosed liabilities.

Representation Type	Example Clause	Risk Addressed
Financial Representation	"All financial statements are accurate and compliant with GAAP."	Prevents misrepresentation of financial health
Legal Compliance	"Company operations comply with applicable laws."	Ensures no hidden regulatory risks

Negotiation Tactics:

- Propose materiality thresholds to limit exposure to minor issues.
- Insist on a survival period for warranties (e.g., 18-24 months post-closing).
- Request seller-provided indemnity insurance for additional protection.

Example Scenario:

- **Context:** Buyer identifies a potential environmental liability.
- **Resolution:** Seller agrees to provide a 24-month warranty and a $2M escrow fund for remediation.

3. Debt Covenants

Key Components:

1. **Positive Covenants:**
    - Actions the borrower agrees to undertake, such as maintaining insurance or providing financial reports.
2. **Negative Covenants:**
    - Restrictions on borrower actions, such as incurring additional debt or selling assets.
3. **Financial Covenants:**
    - Metrics the borrower must meet, such as maintaining a minimum DSCR or leverage ratio.

Covenant Type	Example Clause	Objective
Positive Covenant	Provide quarterly audited financials	Ensures transparency for lenders
Negative Covenant	Restrict additional debt beyond $50M	Limits financial risk
Financial Covenant	Maintain DSCR of 1.5x	Ensures debt repayment capacity

Negotiation Tactics:

- Propose cure periods for covenant breaches to prevent immediate defaults.
- Negotiate flexibility in financial covenants during downturns (e.g., covenant-lite loans).
- Use historical performance to justify less restrictive negative covenants.

Example Scenario:

- **Context:** Lender proposes a DSCR of 2.0x, which buyer deems too restrictive.
- **Resolution:** Buyer negotiates a 1.5x DSCR with a six-month cure period for breaches.

Advanced Negotiation Strategies

1. Building Leverage in Negotiations

- **Preparation:** Conduct extensive due diligence to identify vulnerabilities in the counterparty's position.
- **Alternative Options:** Showcase other financing or acquisition opportunities to strengthen your bargaining position.
- **Psychological Framing:** Present terms as mutually beneficial rather than adversarial.

Leverage Point	Strategy	Outcome
Counterparty Time Pressure	Propose expedited timelines	Achieve faster concessions
Market Comparables	Reference favorable precedents	Secure better pricing terms

Mastering High-Stakes LBO Negotiations

1. **Strategic Negotiation**
   Transform potential LBO opportunities into realized value
2. **Alignment Strategy**
   Meticulously craft purchase agreements, representations, and debt covenants
3. **Negotiation Approach**
   Leverage market intelligence and anticipate potential deadlocks
4. **Investment Performance**
   Engineer negotiation frameworks for sustainable long-term returns

2. Handling Deadlocks

- **Mediation:** Engage neutral third parties to resolve disputes.
- **Trade-Offs:** Concede on lower-priority terms to secure critical provisions.

Example Deadlock:

- **Issue:** Seller refuses to include a MAC clause.
- **Resolution:** Agree to include a narrower MAC clause focused only on regulatory changes.

Negotiation Checklist

Section	Key Question	Action Required
Purchase Agreements	Are working capital adjustments defined clearly?	Establish thresholds and dispute mechanisms.
Representations and Warranties	Are warranties backed by sufficient indemnities?	Propose escrow or insurance coverage.
Debt Covenants	Are covenants flexible enough for downturns?	Negotiate cure periods or covenant-lite structures.

Conclusion

Effective negotiation strategies are essential for aligning deal terms with the objectives of all stakeholders in an LBO. By mastering the art of negotiating purchase agreements, representations and warranties, and debt covenants, participants can mitigate risks, enhance deal value, and foster successful outcomes. Advanced tactics such as leveraging market data and preparing for deadlocks further strengthen negotiation capabilities.

Private Debt – An LBO Perspective

Private debt plays a crucial role in **leveraged buyouts (LBOs)**, providing the financial backbone that allows investors to acquire companies with **minimal equity investment** and **maximum leverage**. Unlike traditional bank loans, **private debt lenders** cater to borrowers with **bespoke financing solutions** tailored for **complex acquisitions, restructurings, and buyouts**.

1. Introduction to Private Debt in LBOs

The demand for **private debt in LBOs** has surged as institutional investors seek **higher yields** and **stable returns** in an environment where traditional bank lending has become more conservative due to **regulatory capital requirements**.

This summary explores **how private debt operates from a borrower's perspective** in the LBO space, covering:

✓ The **structure** of private debt in buyouts.

✓ The **role of private credit funds**.

✓ The **types of debt instruments used**.

✓ The **costs, risks, and covenants** that borrowers must navigate.

2. Understanding Private Debt for LBOs

Private debt funds are alternative lenders that raise capital from **institutional investors, family offices, and pension funds**, then deploy it as direct loans to **mid-to-large private companies**.

Unlike traditional bank financing, private debt funds offer:

✓ **More flexible terms** for LBO borrowers.

✓ **Higher leverage levels** than traditional banks.

✓ **Customized repayment schedules** that align with cash flow cycles.

2.1 Why LBOs Use Private Debt

LBO firms rely on private debt for several reasons:

✓ **Higher debt financing** allows them to **maximize IRR** on equity investments.

✓ **Less restrictive underwriting** compared to commercial banks.

✓ **Quicker execution**, ensuring deals close on time.

✓ **Covenant-lite structures**, reducing borrower restrictions.

2.2 Key Private Debt Providers in LBOs

LBO sponsors typically engage the following **private lenders**:

- **Direct Lending Funds:** Specialize in middle-market buyouts, providing unitranche and mezzanine debt.

- **Private Credit Arms of Investment Firms:** Institutions like Blackstone, Apollo, and KKR have credit divisions catering to LBO financing.
- **Special Situations Funds:** Provide capital for distressed or complex acquisitions.
- **Mezzanine Debt Funds:** Offer subordinated debt with equity participation for high-risk buyouts.

3. Structure of Private Debt in an LBO

LBO financing is structured **in tiers**, with different forms of debt **stacked within the capital structure** to balance risk and return.

3.1 Senior vs. Junior Debt

1. **Senior Debt (Lowest Risk, Lowest Cost)**
    - Typically secured against company assets.
    - First in priority for repayment.
    - Lower interest rates (~6%-10%).
    - Can include **term loans (A & B), revolvers, or asset-backed facilities**.
2. **Junior Debt (Higher Risk, Higher Cost)**
    - **Mezzanine debt:** Sits between senior debt and equity.
    - **Second lien loans:** Subordinated to senior lenders.
    - **Payment-in-kind (PIK) debt:** Defers interest payments, compounding debt.
    - Interest rates can range from **10%-16%**.
3. **Equity Component**
    - Sponsors contribute **10%-30% equity** in LBO deals.
    - In some cases, private debt funds take **warrants or equity kickers** for upside.

3.2 Unitranche Debt: A One-Stop Solution

To simplify capital structures, **unitranche debt** combines **senior and subordinated debt** into a **single facility**. This benefits LBO borrowers by:
✓ Reducing **intercreditor disputes**.

✓ Offering **greater leverage** (~5.5x-6.5x EBITDA).
✓ Providing **faster deal execution**.

4. Cost of Private Debt & Key Terms

While **private debt offers flexibility**, it **comes at a cost**. Borrowers must navigate **interest rates, fees, covenants, and prepayment penalties**.

4.1 Interest Rates & Fees

Private debt pricing depends on:
✓ **Leverage multiples (Debt/EBITDA)** – Higher leverage = higher pricing.
✓ **Risk profile of the target company** – Distressed deals demand higher spreads.
✓ **Market liquidity & investor demand**.

Typical Pricing Ranges:

- **Senior secured loans: SOFR + 5-7%**
- **Mezzanine debt: SOFR + 8-12%** + equity kicker
- **PIK loans: 12-16%** (compounded interest)

Private debt lenders also charge:

✓ **Origination fees (1-3%)** – Upfront cost for structuring the deal.
✓ **Exit/prepayment fees (1-2%)** – Compensation for early repayment.
✓ **Commitment fees (0.5-1%)** – Charged on undrawn amounts.

5. Covenant Structures & Restrictions

Private debt lenders impose **covenants** to protect their downside, though **covenant-lite structures** are more common in sponsor-backed LBOs.

5.1 Financial Covenants

- **Leverage Ratio:** Ensures debt doesn't exceed **X times EBITDA**.
- **Interest Coverage Ratio:** EBITDA must cover interest expense by **Y times**.
- **Debt Service Coverage Ratio:** Protects against cash flow shortfalls.

5.2 Operational Covenants

- **Change of Control:** Prevents unauthorized changes in ownership.
- **Dividend Restrictions:** Limits cash leakage to equity holders.
- **Capital Expenditure Limits:** Controls excessive spending.

LBO sponsors often **negotiate covenant flexibility** in exchange for higher pricing.

6. Risks of Private Debt for LBO Borrowers

While private debt **enables aggressive financing**, it also introduces risks:

1. **High Leverage Risk**
    - Excessive debt loads increase default probability.
2. **Refinancing Risk**
    - Private debt typically matures in **5-7 years**, requiring a refinancing strategy.
3. **Macroeconomic Sensitivity**
    - Rising interest rates can strain cash flows in **floating-rate structures**.
4. **Lender Control & Restrictions**
    - If covenants are breached, lenders can **force renegotiation** or trigger defaults.

Borrowers must **stress-test debt sustainability** under **multiple economic scenarios**.

7. Exit Strategies & Refinancing

LBO sponsors must plan for **debt repayment or refinancing** within the loan maturity period.

7.1 Common Exit Strategies:

✓ **IPO** – Listing the company on the stock exchange.
✓ **Secondary Buyout** – Selling to another PE firm.
✓ **Trade Sale** – Selling to a strategic acquirer.
✓ **Debt Refinancing** – Replacing old debt with cheaper long-term financing.

7.2 Deleveraging Over Time

✓ LBO firms use **cash flows** to **pay down debt** and improve creditworthiness.
✓ Some sponsors **roll over** private debt into **cheaper bank loans** post-acquisition.

Anatomy of an SPA

This appendix provides an in-depth exploration of the Sales and Purchase Agreement (SPA) – the critical legal document that governs the sale and acquisition of a business. The SPA is a complex, detail-rich contract that outlines each party's rights, obligations, and the conditions required for a successful transaction. Its careful construction is key to ensuring that both buyer and seller are protected and that the deal proceeds smoothly.

Introduction

A **Sale and Purchase Agreement (SPA)** is the definitive, legally binding contract that governs the terms and conditions of a business acquisition. It is a crucial document in any **Mergers and Acquisitions (M&A)** transaction, ensuring that both the buyer and the seller are legally protected and that all elements of the deal are explicitly documented.

The SPA is **not a simple agreement**; it is a **highly detailed and structured contract** that requires precision. A single paragraph can be the difference between a successful transaction and legal disputes. Its construction must take into account various financial, operational, and legal considerations.

SPAs differ depending on the nature of the transaction. For example:

- **Asset Purchases** – Only specific assets and liabilities are transferred.
- **Stock Purchases** – Ownership of the entire entity is transferred.
- **Auctions** – A standardized SPA is issued to all bidders, and modifications are proposed by the highest bidder.

Regardless of the structure, every SPA follows a similar **anatomy**, which this appendix explores in detail.

1. Preamble & Recitals

The **Preamble** introduces the agreement and sets the foundation for the contractual obligations outlined in later sections. It typically contains **"Recitals"**, which explain the background and intent of the transaction.

1.1 Identification of the Parties

The SPA begins by formally identifying:

1. The **Buyer** (Purchaser), including the name, registered address, and corporate details.
2. The **Seller**, identifying whether it is an individual, a private company, a holding entity, or a publicly listed firm.
3. Any **third parties**, such as guarantors, debt providers, or parent entities, that are integral to the execution of the agreement.

Example of Party Identification Clause:

"This Sale and Purchase Agreement is made and entered into on [Date], by and between [BUYER'S NAME], a corporation organized and existing under the laws of [Country/State], with

its principal place of business located at [Address] (hereinafter referred to as "Buyer"), and [SELLER'S NAME], a corporation duly incorporated and registered in [Country/State], with its principal place of business located at [Address] (hereinafter referred to as "Seller")."

1.2 Description of the Transaction

This section provides a high-level summary of the intended sale, including:

- Whether it is a **share purchase agreement** (sale of the company's stock/equity) or an **asset purchase agreement** (sale of specific business assets).
- The **purchase price** or **consideration** to be paid.
- A basic description of the **business or assets being transferred**.
- A reference to key steps taken before the SPA, such as **due diligence** and prior agreements like a Letter of Intent (LOI) or a Memorandum of Understanding (MOU).

Example of Transaction Summary Clause:

"WHEREAS, the Seller is engaged in the business of [Business Description], and the Buyer desires to acquire from the Seller all of the issued and outstanding shares of [Company Name] (the "Company"), in accordance with the terms and conditions set forth herein. The Seller agrees to transfer the full ownership of the Company, including all assets and liabilities, to the Buyer for the agreed consideration of [Purchase Price]."

1.3 Corporate Approvals & Shareholder Consent

- If the company being sold is **privately held**, all shareholders must sign the SPA or issue formal consent.
- If the company is **publicly traded**, the transaction might require approval from a **Board of Directors**, regulatory bodies, or **shareholder voting** under corporate governance laws.

This section clarifies:

- **Who has the authority to sign the SPA** on behalf of the Buyer and Seller.
- **Whether board approvals, shareholder approvals, or regulatory clearances are needed** before the transaction closes.

Example of Approval Clause:

"The Seller represents and warrants that it has obtained all necessary corporate approvals, including the authorization of its Board of Directors and majority shareholders, to execute and deliver this Agreement. The execution of this SPA will not conflict with or result in any violation of the governing documents of the Seller or any applicable laws."

2. Subject of Sale

The **Subject of Sale** clause specifies what is being sold and transferred under the agreement. It should **eliminate any ambiguity** about the transaction scope.

- **In a Stock Purchase Agreement (SPA):** This section states that the Buyer is acquiring a specified number of shares in the target company, including all rights, obligations, and liabilities attached to those shares.
- **In an Asset Purchase Agreement (APA):** This section lists **exactly which assets are being transferred**, such as real estate, machinery, patents, intellectual property, inventory, and contracts.

2.1 Detailed Asset/Business Description

The SPA must **clearly define the nature of the assets or shares** included in the deal. It may reference annexes that contain a **full inventory list, financials, or legal descriptions** of the property.

Example of Subject of Sale Clause:

"The Seller agrees to sell, and the Buyer agrees to purchase, 100% of the issued and outstanding shares of [Company Name] (the "Company"), free and clear of any encumbrances, liens, or third-party claims, as of the Closing Date."

Or, in the case of an **Asset Sale:**

*"The Seller agrees to sell and transfer to the Buyer, and the Buyer agrees to purchase, the following assets of the Business:

1. All inventory and stock listed in Schedule A.
2. All tangible fixed assets, including machinery, equipment, and office furniture, as listed in Schedule B.
3. All intellectual property rights, including patents, trademarks, copyrights, and domain names, as listed in Schedule C.
4. All customer contracts, supplier agreements, and employment agreements that the Buyer has elected to assume."*

Clarifications Required in the SPA:

- **Excluded Assets:** The agreement should explicitly state if any assets are **not included** in the sale.
- **Assumed Liabilities:** If the Buyer is taking responsibility for specific debts or obligations, these should be itemized in an annex.

- **Retention of Certain Rights:** If the Seller retains certain rights (e.g., licensing of intellectual property), these must be clearly defined.

3. Purchase Price & Payment Terms

The **Purchase Price & Payment Terms** section outlines:
✓ The **total price** for the business or assets.
✓ How and when **payment will be made**.
✓ Any **price adjustments, escrows, holdbacks, or earn-outs**.

A well-structured **payment mechanism** protects both parties from financial risks.

3.1 Purchase Price Structure

The price may be **fixed** or **variable**, depending on:

- **Upfront lump sum payments** (common in straightforward deals).
- **Deferred payments** spread over months or years.
- **Earn-out provisions**, where additional amounts are paid if financial performance targets are met.
- **Stock-for-stock transactions**, where shares in the acquiring company are exchanged for the seller's shares.

Example of Purchase Price Clause:

*"The Buyer shall pay the Seller a total consideration of $[X], which shall be payable in the following manner:

1. An initial cash payment of $[X] upon Closing.
2. A deferred payment of $[X] to be paid within [X] months after Closing.
3. An earn-out payment of up to $[X], contingent on the Company achieving an EBITDA of $[X] within [X] years."*

3.2 Price Adjustments

Price adjustments are used when the final price depends on **future financial conditions**, such as:

- **Working Capital Adjustments** – Ensuring the company's balance sheet remains stable at closing.
- **Debt & Cash Adjustments** – The buyer typically deducts **net debt** from the purchase price.

- **Post-Closing Adjustments** – Reconciliation of financials within a set period (e.g., 90 days).

Example of Price Adjustment Clause:

"The Purchase Price shall be subject to adjustment based on the net working capital of the Company as of the Closing Date. If the final net working capital exceeds the Target Amount of $[X], the Buyer shall pay the Seller the excess amount. If the final net working capital is lower than the Target Amount, the Seller shall refund the deficit."

3.3 Payment Methods

The SPA should clearly specify how payments will be made:

✓ **Wire transfers to designated bank accounts**.

✓ **Escrow arrangements**, where funds are temporarily held by a neutral third party.

✓ **Promissory notes** if part of the payment is deferred.

4. Preceding Conditions (Closing Conditions)

Preceding conditions (also known as **Conditions Precedent**) are requirements that must be fulfilled before the deal **officially closes**.

4.1 Typical Closing Conditions:

- **Regulatory Approvals:**
    - Government or antitrust approvals.
    - Sector-specific licenses (e.g., financial or healthcare companies).
- **Third-Party Consents:**
    - Approval from existing lenders, suppliers, or landlords.
- **Debt Repayments:**
    - Any outstanding liabilities must be cleared before the transfer.
- **Operational Conditions:**
    - The company must operate "in the ordinary course of business" until closing.

Example of Preceding Conditions Clause:

*"The obligation of the Buyer to proceed with the Closing shall be subject to the satisfaction of the following conditions:

1. Receipt of all necessary regulatory approvals.
2. No material adverse change has occurred in the financial condition of the Company.
3. The Seller has provided evidence of debt repayment and all required third-party consents."*

5. Representations & Warranties

Representations and Warranties (R&W) are **legally binding statements** made by both parties about the business. If any statement is false, the affected party may claim damages.

5.1 Seller's Representations & Warranties

The Seller confirms that:
✓ The company **owns all of its assets** and has **no undisclosed liabilities**.
✓ The **financial statements are accurate**.
✓ There are **no pending lawsuits** or regulatory violations.
✓ All intellectual property (IP), contracts, and key assets **are legally valid**.

Example of Seller's Representations & Warranties Clause:

*"The Seller represents and warrants that:

1. The Company's audited financial statements for the past three years fairly present its financial condition.
2. The Company owns or has valid rights to all intellectual property necessary for its operations.
3. The Company is not engaged in any pending or threatened litigation that would materially impact its financial standing."*

5.2 Buyer's Representations & Warranties

The Buyer confirms that:
✓ It **has the legal and financial capacity** to complete the transaction.
✓ The **funding arrangements** are in place.
✓ There are **no hidden conflicts of interest**.

Example of Buyer's Representations & Warranties Clause:

*"The Buyer represents and warrants that:

1. It has sufficient funds and the necessary corporate approvals to complete the transaction.
2. The execution and delivery of this Agreement do not violate any applicable laws or agreements to which the Buyer is a party.
3. There are no current or pending investigations that would affect the Buyer's ability to fulfill its obligations under this Agreement."*

5.3 Survival of Representations & Warranties

- Most R&W clauses **expire after a set period**, typically **12 to 24 months** after closing.
- Certain warranties, such as **tax liabilities and environmental claims**, may survive for **5-7 years**.

Example of Survival Clause:

"The representations and warranties contained in this Agreement shall remain in full force and effect for a period of 18 months from the Closing Date, except for tax-related representations, which shall survive for a period of 5 years."

6. Closing & Post-Closing Obligations

The **Closing** is the final step in executing the Sale and Purchase Agreement (SPA). It is when the ownership of shares or assets is officially transferred, and the Buyer completes payment.

6.1 Closing Process

The SPA specifies:
✓ **Closing Date:** The exact date when all conditions precedent must be satisfied.
✓ **Location & Method:** Whether closing is in person, via electronic exchange, or in escrow.
✓ **Final Documentation:** List of documents to be exchanged, such as share certificates, resignation letters of directors, financial statements, and board resolutions.

Example of Closing Clause:

"The Closing of the transaction shall take place at the offices of [Designated Law Firm] on [Closing Date] at [Time], or at such other place and time as mutually agreed by the Parties. At Closing, the Buyer shall deliver the Purchase Price as per the agreed payment schedule, and the Seller shall deliver all necessary transfer documentation, including stock certificates, regulatory approvals, and corporate resolutions."

6.2 Deliverables at Closing

The SPA typically includes an annex listing documents required at Closing:

- **From the Seller:**
  ✓ Share transfer agreements or asset transfer deeds.
  ✓ Updated financial statements.
  ✓ Resignation letters of directors and officers (if applicable).
  ✓ Evidence of debt repayments (if required).
- **From the Buyer:**
  ✓ Payment confirmation or escrow instructions.
  ✓ Regulatory approvals or licenses.
  ✓ Board resolutions approving the transaction.

6.3 Post-Closing Obligations

After the transaction is finalized, additional obligations may remain:

- **Integration and Transition Support:** The Seller may agree to assist for a fixed period.
- **Employee Transfers:** If the business includes employees, employment contracts must be honored.
- **Regulatory Filings:** Some jurisdictions require formal government notifications after a business sale.

7. Indemnities & Risk Allocation

Indemnities protect the Buyer from financial losses resulting from undisclosed liabilities, contract breaches, or other post-closing risks.

7.1 Purpose of Indemnities

✓ **Protect the Buyer** if the Seller made false representations.
✓ **Cover financial risks** such as tax liabilities, environmental issues, or pending litigation.
✓ **Allocate liability** based on specific risk areas.

7.2 Types of Indemnities

1. **General Indemnities:** Broad protections covering breaches of the agreement.
2. **Specific Indemnities:** Focused on known risks identified during due diligence (e.g., pending tax audits).
3. **Tax Indemnities:** Ensure that pre-closing tax liabilities remain the Seller's responsibility.

Example of Indemnity Clause:

"The Seller agrees to indemnify and hold harmless the Buyer against any and all losses, damages, claims, and expenses (including reasonable legal fees) arising from:
(i) any breach of the representations and warranties contained in this Agreement;
(ii) any undisclosed liabilities existing prior to the Closing Date; and
(iii) any failure to comply with tax obligations for periods before Closing."

7.3 Indemnity Limits & Timeframes

- **Survival Period:** Indemnities typically survive for **12-24 months** post-closing, except tax-related indemnities, which can last **5-7 years**.
- **Caps & Thresholds:** The SPA may set a **maximum liability cap** or a **minimum threshold** before indemnities apply.

Example of Indemnity Cap Clause:

"The Seller's total liability under this indemnity provision shall not exceed [X]% of the Purchase Price, except for claims arising from fraud or willful misconduct, which shall have no cap."

8. Confidentiality & Non-Compete Agreements

8.1 Confidentiality Obligations

Most SPAs include a **confidentiality clause** to protect sensitive business information, trade secrets, and deal terms.

✓ Prevents disclosure of proprietary data.

✓ Ensures that negotiations and financial details remain private.

✓ Typically lasts **2-5 years** after the deal.

Example of Confidentiality Clause:

"Both parties agree to maintain the confidentiality of all proprietary business information obtained during the negotiation and execution of this Agreement. This obligation shall survive for a period of [X] years following the Closing Date."

8.2 Non-Compete & Non-Solicitation Clauses

To prevent unfair competition, the SPA may restrict the Seller from:

✓ Competing with the Buyer for a defined **period and geography**.

✓ Soliciting former **clients, suppliers, or employees**.

Example of Non-Compete Clause:

"The Seller agrees that for a period of [X] years following the Closing Date, it shall not engage in any business that directly competes with the acquired business within [Geographic Area]."

✓ **Time Limit:** Typically **1-5 years**, depending on jurisdiction.

✓ **Scope Limit:** Must be **reasonable** under competition laws.

9. Governing Law & Dispute Resolution

9.1 Choice of Law

✓ Specifies which **country's or state's laws** will govern the SPA.
✓ Important for cross-border deals where different legal frameworks apply.

Example of Governing Law Clause:

"This Agreement shall be governed by and construed in accordance with the laws of [Jurisdiction]."

9.2 Dispute Resolution Methods

Disputes may be resolved through:

1. **Negotiation & Mediation:**
    - Requires both parties to attempt **good faith** negotiations before legal action.
2. **Arbitration:**
    - Common in **international transactions** to avoid lengthy court cases.
    - Faster and **private** compared to litigation.
3. **Litigation:**
    - Court action under the chosen **governing law**.
    - Often a **last resort** due to high costs and time delays.

Example of Arbitration Clause:

"Any disputes arising out of or related to this Agreement shall be resolved by arbitration in [City, Country], in accordance with the rules of [Arbitration Institution]. The decision of the arbitrator(s) shall be final and binding upon the parties."

9.3 Remedies for Breach

The SPA should specify **consequences** if either party violates its obligations:
✓ Financial penalties for contract breaches.
✓ Specific performance clauses (e.g., forcing the Seller to complete an obligation).

Example of Remedies Clause:

"In the event of a material breach, the non-breaching party shall be entitled to seek injunctive relief, specific performance, or damages as provided under applicable law."

10. Miscellaneous Provisions

SPAs often contain a **"boilerplate" section** with additional legal protections:

✓ **Entire Agreement:** Confirms that no other verbal or written agreements exist.

✓ **Severability Clause:** Ensures that if one clause is invalid, the rest of the SPA remains enforceable.

✓ **Force Majeure:** Protects against obligations if unexpected events (e.g., wars, natural disasters) disrupt the deal.

Example of Entire Agreement Clause:

"This Agreement constitutes the entire understanding between the Parties and supersedes all prior agreements, whether written or oral, relating to the subject matter herein."

PRACTICE TESTS

Practice Test 1

Questions

1. What is the primary objective of a leveraged buyout (LBO)?

   a. Liquidating non-core assets
   b. Achieving high returns through operational improvements and leverage
   c. Diversifying across multiple industries
   d. Maximizing dividend payouts immediately

2. Which financial metric is commonly used to evaluate a company's operational profitability before interest and taxes?
   a. Free Cash Flow
   b. EBITDA
   c. Gross Margin
   d. Net Income

3. What distinguishes mezzanine debt in LBO financing?
   a. It is secured by the company's assets
   b. It often includes equity kickers or warrants
   c. It is interest-free
   d. It has the lowest cost of capital

4. Why are ESG factors becoming critical in private equity investments?
   a. To eliminate the need for financial reporting
   b. To align with investor expectations for sustainability and ethical practices
   c. To focus exclusively on renewable energy companies
   d. To reduce regulatory compliance requirements

5. Which of the following best describes a dual-track exit strategy?
   a. Selling equity to multiple private equity firms
   b. Simultaneously preparing for an IPO and a strategic sale
   c. Conducting two IPOs for the same portfolio company
   d. Delaying exit strategies indefinitely

6. How does a bullet repayment schedule impact LBO cash flows?
   a. It eliminates interest payments
   b. It defers principal repayment until maturity
   c. It prioritizes equity payouts over debt servicing
   d. It reduces overall leverage requirements

7. What is the significance of a management incentive plan in an LBO?
   a. To minimize operational oversight
   b. To align management goals with those of the financial sponsor
   c. To reduce employee turnover in non-core divisions
   d. To enhance dividend distributions
8. Which scenario represents operational value creation in an LBO portfolio company?
   a. Increasing leverage ratios to refinance debt
   b. Streamlining manufacturing processes to improve margins
   c. Diversifying into unrelated industries
   d. Selling core assets to reduce liabilities
9. What role does predictive analytics play in modern private equity operations?
   a. It replaces the need for due diligence
   b. It forecasts financial and operational risks
   c. It eliminates regulatory requirements
   d. It focuses solely on historical performance
10. Which type of private equity fund is most likely to invest in companies undergoing financial distress?
    a. Growth equity fund
    b. Venture capital fund
    c. Distressed asset fund
    d. Buyout fund
11. What is the purpose of debt covenants in LBO financing agreements?
    a. To restrict operational flexibility
    b. To ensure compliance with agreed-upon financial metrics
    c. To increase leverage capacity
    d. To eliminate the need for equity contributions
12. Why is multiple expansion critical in private equity exits?
    a. It reduces the need for operational improvements
    b. It allows portfolio companies to avoid capital gains taxes
    c. It enhances exit valuation by achieving a higher EBITDA multiple
    d. It focuses exclusively on dividend payouts
13. How does a covenant-lite loan benefit an LBO sponsor?
    a. It eliminates debt servicing requirements
    b. It provides more operational flexibility by reducing restrictions
    c. It ensures early repayment of debt
    d. It reduces equity contribution requirements

14. What is a key risk in cross-border LBOs?
    a. Limited access to equity financing
    b. Regulatory challenges and currency fluctuations
    c. Excessive operational control by lenders
    d. Reduced free cash flow generation

15. Which financial metric measures the efficiency of converting EBITDA into cash flow?
    a. Gross Margin
    b. Free Cash Flow Conversion
    c. Debt-to-Equity Ratio
    d. IRR

16. What is the primary role of operating partners in LBO value creation?
    a. Providing capital for the transaction
    b. Driving operational improvements in portfolio companies
    c. Managing investor relations
    d. Structuring debt financing packages

17. How does tokenization benefit private equity investments?
    a. It eliminates regulatory compliance
    b. It enhances liquidity through fractional ownership
    c. It reduces the need for financial modeling
    d. It eliminates operational oversight

18. Which exit strategy typically achieves the highest valuation multiples?
    a. Recapitalization
    b. Trade sale
    c. Secondary sale
    d. Initial Public Offering (IPO)

19. What is a key benefit of using unitranche debt in LBO financing?
    a. Simplified structure combining senior and subordinated debt
    b. Reduced need for financial covenants
    c. Interest-free repayment schedules
    d. Increased regulatory flexibility

20. Why is scenario planning critical in LBO modeling?
    a. To eliminate the need for stress testing
    b. To evaluate the impact of varying assumptions on deal outcomes
    c. To avoid equity dilution
    d. To reduce due diligence timelines

21. What distinguishes growth equity from other forms of private equity investing?
    a. Focuses on early-stage startups exclusively

b. Targets companies with significant growth potential and limited debt
c. Avoids operational improvements
d. Invests in companies on the verge of liquidation

22. Which metric is used to measure the proportion of debt to EBITDA?
    a. Leverage Ratio
    b. Dividend Yield
    c. Free Cash Flow Conversion
    d. Price-to-Earnings Ratio

23. How does AI-driven due diligence enhance LBO deal sourcing?
    a. By eliminating manual research entirely
    b. By identifying high-potential targets through advanced data analysis
    c. By automating operational improvements
    d. By increasing the speed of financial modeling

24. What is the main challenge of integrating ESG metrics into portfolio companies?
    a. Increased liquidity risks
    b. Higher compliance costs and implementation complexities
    c. Reduced operational control by sponsors
    d. Eliminating traditional financial reporting

25. What is the primary advantage of thematic funds in private equity?
    a. Exclusively investing in distressed companies
    b. Focusing on emerging trends like AI and climate tech
    c. Reducing the need for portfolio diversification
    d. Eliminating compliance requirements

26. Why is cultural alignment important in post-acquisition integration?
    a. To simplify financial reporting
    b. To ensure collaboration between existing and new leadership
    c. To prioritize dividend payouts
    d. To reduce operational complexities

27. What is a common goal during the exit planning stage in an LBO?
    a. Minimizing due diligence requirements
    b. Timing the exit to maximize investor returns
    c. Eliminating operational improvements
    d. Avoiding all external regulatory filings

28. How does digital transformation drive value creation in portfolio companies?
    a. By replacing leadership teams
    b. By enhancing operational efficiency and customer engagement

c. By eliminating traditional debt structures
d. By avoiding regulatory compliance entirely

29. Which leadership style is best suited for driving innovation in portfolio companies?
    a. Bureaucratic leadership
    b. Transformational leadership
    c. Authoritative leadership
    d. Autocratic leadership

30. What is the primary purpose of an investment thesis in private equity?
    a. To define the fund's target sectors and strategies
    b. To reduce the need for financial modeling
    c. To focus exclusively on early-stage companies
    d. To eliminate operational complexities

Answer Key

1. b
2. b
3. b
4. b
5. b
6. b
7. b
8. b
9. b
10. c
11. b
12. c
13. b
14. b
15. b
16. b
17. b
18. d
19. a
20. b
21. b
22. a
23. b
24. b
25. b
26. b

27. b

28. b

29. b

30. a

Practice Test 2

Questions

1. What is the primary focus of value creation in private equity?
   a. Maximizing dividend payouts
   b. Enhancing operational and financial performance
   c. Increasing debt levels
   d. Expanding into unrelated industries

2. Which stage in the LBO lifecycle involves sourcing potential targets?
   a. Exit strategy
   b. Fundraising
   c. Deal origination
   d. Operational improvement

3. What is a key benefit of incorporating ESG metrics into portfolio management?
   a. Avoiding regulatory compliance
   b. Attracting socially conscious investors
   c. Eliminating due diligence requirements
   d. Reducing operational oversight

4. Which debt instrument is most likely to include equity warrants as part of its structure?
   a. Senior debt
   b. Mezzanine debt
   c. High-yield bonds
   d. Convertible debt

5. What is the role of financial modeling in an LBO?
   a. To eliminate operational inefficiencies
   b. To project cash flows and assess deal feasibility
   c. To determine exit timing exclusively
   d. To replace due diligence processes

6. Which technology is most commonly used for real-time performance tracking in private equity?
   a. Blockchain
   b. Artificial Intelligence (AI)
   c. Internet of Things (IoT)
   d. Robotic Process Automation (RPA)

7. How does free cash flow (FCF) impact LBO success?
   a. It ensures consistent dividend payouts
   b. It is used to service debt and fund operational improvements
   c. It eliminates the need for equity financing
   d. It measures company profitability before interest and taxes

8. What distinguishes growth equity from venture capital?
   a. Growth equity targets startups with no revenue
   b. Growth equity focuses on scaling established companies
   c. Growth equity avoids operational involvement
   d. Growth equity is exclusively for technology companies

9. Which metric is commonly used to evaluate the profitability of a portfolio company post-acquisition?
   a. Net income
   b. EBITDA margin
   c. Leverage ratio
   d. Dividend yield

10. What is a common risk in using high-yield bonds for LBO financing?
   a. Lack of operational flexibility
   b. High default risk due to unsecured nature
   c. Excessive equity dilution
   d. Limited market access

11. Why is digital transformation important for portfolio companies?
   a. To eliminate regulatory reporting
   b. To enhance efficiency and customer engagement
   c. To reduce employee headcount
   d. To avoid market competition

12. What is the primary purpose of a secondary sale in private equity?
   a. Selling a portfolio company to another private equity firm
   b. Conducting an IPO
   c. Issuing new equity to retail investors
   d. Refinancing existing debt

13. Which financial metric measures the ability to cover debt obligations?
   a. Debt Service Coverage Ratio (DSCR)
   b. Free Cash Flow Conversion
   c. Internal Rate of Return (IRR)
   d. Total Value to Paid-In (TVPI)

14. How do transformational leaders create value in private equity?
    a. By focusing on short-term cost-cutting measures
    b. By driving innovation and inspiring organizational change
    c. By avoiding operational involvement
    d. By increasing financial leverage exclusively

15. What is the primary goal of distressed asset investing in private equity?
    a. Scaling high-growth companies
    b. Acquiring undervalued companies for turnaround
    c. Avoiding operational restructuring
    d. Eliminating existing liabilities

16. Why is an investment thesis important in LBO execution?
    a. It defines the fund's strategy and target sectors
    b. It eliminates the need for due diligence
    c. It focuses exclusively on market trends
    d. It prioritizes equity dilution

17. Which metric is used to calculate the proportion of equity returns relative to total capital invested?
    a. IRR
    b. Return on Equity (ROE)
    c. Cash-on-Cash Return
    d. Earnings Per Share (EPS)

18. What is a thematic fund in private equity?
    a. A fund focusing on specific trends or sectors
    b. A general-purpose investment fund
    c. A fund targeting early-stage startups
    d. A fund avoiding ESG integration

19. What is a common characteristic of unitranche debt in LBOs?
    a. It combines senior and subordinated debt into a single structure
    b. It is exclusively interest-free
    c. It avoids all covenant requirements
    d. It reduces equity contributions entirely

20. How does predictive analytics benefit LBO post-acquisition monitoring?
    a. By forecasting potential risks and trends
    b. By eliminating manual reporting processes
    c. By focusing solely on historical performance
    d. By replacing all operational leadership

21. Which leadership style emphasizes collaboration and team development in portfolio companies?
    a. Transformational leadership
    b. Servant leadership
    c. Autocratic leadership
    d. Bureaucratic leadership

22. Why is liquidity management critical in LBOs?
    a. To increase dividend payouts
    b. To ensure sufficient cash flow for debt servicing
    c. To eliminate the need for equity contributions
    d. To prioritize leverage ratios

23. What is the significance of a value creation plan in private equity?
    a. It defines operational and financial improvements post-acquisition
    b. It eliminates the need for board oversight
    c. It focuses exclusively on equity returns
    d. It reduces regulatory compliance requirements

24. Which metric is used to measure operational efficiency in portfolio companies?
    a. Gross Margin
    b. EBITDA Margin
    c. Net Income
    d. Dividend Yield

25. Why is stakeholder alignment important in LBOs?
    a. To prioritize operational inefficiencies
    b. To ensure collaboration between sponsors, management, and lenders
    c. To avoid board involvement
    d. To reduce free cash flow generation

26. What is the role of scenario analysis in LBO modeling?
    a. To eliminate equity dilution
    b. To assess deal outcomes under varying conditions
    c. To simplify financial projections
    d. To prioritize debt covenants

27. Which technology is commonly used to enhance deal sourcing?
    a. Predictive analytics and machine learning
    b. Blockchain smart contracts
    c. Manual market analysis
    d. Traditional CRM systems

28. How does cultural alignment contribute to successful post-acquisition integration?
    a. By simplifying financial modeling
    b. By fostering collaboration between leadership teams
    c. By eliminating operational inefficiencies
    d. By reducing free cash flow requirements
29. What is a key advantage of thematic investing in private equity?
    a. It focuses on speculative startups
    b. It aligns investment strategies with emerging trends
    c. It avoids all compliance requirements
    d. It prioritizes short-term gains exclusively
30. What is the ultimate goal of an LBO exit strategy?
    a. To reduce operational oversight
    b. To maximize investor returns through a strategic sale or IPO
    c. To prioritize debt servicing
    d. To eliminate regulatory reporting

Answer Key

1. b
2. c
3. b
4. b
5. b
6. b
7. b
8. b
9. b
10. b
11. b
12. a
13. a
14. b
15. b
16. a
17. c
18. a
19. a
20. a
21. b
22. b
23. a
24. b
25. b
26. b

27. a

28. b

29. b

30. b

Practice Test 3

Questions

1. What is the primary benefit of portfolio optimization in private equity?
   a. Improving cash flow for reinvestment
   b. Reducing compliance costs
   c. Eliminating operational inefficiencies
   d. Achieving diversification across industries

2. How does an earn-out clause function in a private equity purchase agreement?
   a. Defers payment based on future performance milestones
   b. Avoids equity dilution during acquisitions
   c. Ensures full payment at the time of acquisition
   d. Caps the seller's liability to fixed amounts

3. What distinguishes mezzanine financing from other types of debt?
   a. It is always secured by assets
   b. It combines debt and equity features
   c. It carries the lowest interest rates
   d. It avoids repayment until maturity

4. Which metric evaluates a portfolio company's ability to convert sales into cash?
   a. Free Cash Flow Conversion
   b. Return on Equity (ROE)
   c. EBITDA Margin
   d. Debt-to-Equity Ratio

5. What is a primary advantage of using tokenization in private equity?
   a. Reducing the need for physical assets
   b. Enhancing liquidity through fractional ownership
   c. Eliminating operational oversight
   d. Avoiding regulatory compliance

6. How do subscription lines of credit benefit private equity funds?
   a. By reducing equity contributions from investors
   b. By bridging timing gaps between capital calls
   c. By eliminating the need for due diligence
   d. By prioritizing dividend payouts

7. Which metric is commonly used to measure the risk-adjusted returns of a private equity investment?
   a. Sharpe Ratio

b. Cash-on-Cash Return
c. Internal Rate of Return (IRR)
d. Total Value to Paid-In (TVPI)

8. Why is leadership alignment critical during post-acquisition integration?
   a. To avoid equity dilution
   b. To ensure clear communication and shared strategic goals
   c. To reduce operational oversight
   d. To simplify financial reporting

9. What is a secondary buyout in private equity?
   a. Selling a portfolio company to another private equity firm
   b. Conducting a recapitalization within the same firm
   c. Issuing new equity to retail investors
   d. Merging two portfolio companies

10. How does AI-driven due diligence transform deal sourcing?
    a. By automating the identification of high-potential targets
    b. By eliminating the need for legal reviews
    c. By prioritizing short-term profitability
    d. By avoiding compliance-related issues

11. Which characteristic best describes transformational leadership in private equity?
    a. Prioritizing short-term financial goals
    b. Driving innovation and inspiring organizational change
    c. Reducing employee engagement
    d. Focusing solely on cost-cutting measures

12. What is the primary purpose of a bridge loan in private equity?
    a. To provide interim financing for acquisitions
    b. To replace existing debt
    c. To fund operational improvements
    d. To reduce equity dilution

13. Which stage of the LBO lifecycle focuses on operational value creation?
    a. Deal sourcing
    b. Exit planning
    c. Post-acquisition management
    d. Fundraising

14. Why is multiple expansion significant in private equity exits?
    a. It reduces operational risks
    b. It increases the valuation at the time of sale

c. It eliminates debt obligations
d. It prioritizes cash flow generation

15. How does cultural alignment influence portfolio company performance post-acquisition?
    a. By fostering collaboration between management and sponsors
    b. By reducing reporting requirements
    c. By eliminating operational inefficiencies
    d. By avoiding market expansion strategies

16. What is the primary objective of thematic private equity funds?
    a. Targeting high-growth trends or niche industries
    b. Avoiding ESG integration
    c. Simplifying deal structuring
    d. Prioritizing dividend payouts

17. Which financial metric measures the ratio of debt to EBITDA?
    a. Price-to-Earnings Ratio (P/E)
    b. Leverage Ratio
    c. Dividend Yield
    d. Free Cash Flow Conversion

18. How do sustainability-linked loans (SLLs) align with ESG objectives?
    a. By reducing regulatory oversight
    b. By incentivizing ESG performance with interest rate adjustments
    c. By eliminating debt repayment requirements
    d. By avoiding compliance-related costs

19. What is the significance of an equity bridge in LBO deal structuring?
    a. To align funding with operational improvements
    b. To manage timing gaps between equity contributions and closing
    c. To eliminate the need for senior debt
    d. To prioritize dividend payouts

20. How does free cash flow (FCF) contribute to debt servicing in LBOs?
    a. By enhancing operational flexibility
    b. By funding principal repayments and interest
    c. By reducing equity ownership
    d. By eliminating leverage requirements

21. Why is stakeholder alignment important during an LBO exit?
    a. To reduce investor participation
    b. To ensure smooth execution and maximize returns
    c. To prioritize compliance obligations
    d. To minimize operational improvements

22. What is a distinguishing feature of unitranche financing?
    a. Combining senior and subordinated debt into a single structure
    b. Avoiding financial covenants entirely
    c. Reducing interest rates for mezzanine debt
    d. Eliminating the need for equity contributions

23. How does predictive analytics enhance operational monitoring in portfolio companies?
    a. By forecasting risks and optimizing performance
    b. By replacing all manual processes
    c. By avoiding reporting obligations
    d. By focusing solely on cost reduction

24. Why is scenario planning critical in LBO modeling?
    a. To eliminate uncertainty in deal execution
    b. To evaluate the impact of varying assumptions on outcomes
    c. To prioritize cash-on-cash returns
    d. To reduce leverage ratios

25. What is the primary goal of an LBO exit strategy?
    a. To maximize investor returns through strategic sales or IPOs
    b. To avoid regulatory filings
    c. To eliminate operational inefficiencies
    d. To reduce compliance-related costs

26. Which technology is most commonly used to streamline due diligence processes?
    a. Blockchain
    b. Artificial Intelligence (AI)
    c. Internet of Things (IoT)
    d. Robotic Process Automation (RPA)

27. How does digital transformation create value in portfolio companies?
    a. By enhancing operational efficiency and customer engagement
    b. By eliminating compliance requirements
    c. By prioritizing short-term profitability
    d. By replacing leadership teams entirely

28. Which leadership style is most effective in driving innovation post-acquisition?
    a. Bureaucratic leadership
    b. Transformational leadership
    c. Servant leadership
    d. Autocratic leadership

29. How does cultural misalignment impact post-acquisition performance?
    a. By reducing collaboration and operational efficiency

b. By prioritizing financial performance exclusively
c. By streamlining decision-making processes
d. By enhancing cost-saving measures

30. What is a common characteristic of distressed asset investing in private equity?
a. Targeting companies with high debt and turnaround potential
b. Avoiding operational restructuring entirely
c. Prioritizing dividend payouts over growth
d. Eliminating market expansion strategies

Answer Key

1. b
2. b
3. b
4. a
5. b
6. b
7. a
8. b
9. a
10. a
11. b
12. a
13. c
14. b
15. a
16. a
17. b
18. b
19. b
20. b
21. b
22. a
23. a
24. b
25. a
26. b

27. a

28. b

29. a

30. a

APPENDIX

Comprehensive Glossary of LBO Terms

A

Acquisition Debt: Debt used to finance the purchase of a company. Often secured by the assets or cash flows of the target.

Amortization: The process of gradually paying off debt in regular installments over a specified period.

B

Base Case: A financial scenario that represents the most likely outcome based on historical data and reasonable projections.

Bullet Payment: A lump sum repayment of the principal amount of a loan, typically made at maturity.

Buyout Fund: A type of private equity fund focused on acquiring control of companies through leveraged buyouts.

C

Capital Structure: The mix of debt, equity, and other financial instruments used to finance a company's operations or acquisition.

Cash-on-Cash Return: A measure of equity returns, calculated as the total cash inflows divided by the equity invested.

Covenant: A provision in a loan agreement designed to protect the lender by restricting the borrower's actions (e.g., leverage covenants).

Credit Risk Transfer: Techniques like securitization or syndicated loans used to distribute debt risk among multiple parties.

D

Debt Service Coverage Ratio (DSCR): A financial metric that compares a company's operating income to its debt obligations, indicating its ability to service debt.

Discount Rate: The rate used to calculate the present value of future cash flows in valuation models like DCF.

Due Diligence: A comprehensive appraisal of a target company's financial, legal, and operational status before finalizing an acquisition.

E

EBITDA (Earnings Before Interest, Taxes, Depreciation, and Amortization): A key measure of operational performance, often used as a proxy for cash flow.

Enterprise Value (EV): The total value of a company, including equity and debt, minus cash. A comprehensive measure of a company's valuation.

Equity Contribution: The portion of the acquisition cost funded by the buyer's own equity.

F

Free Cash Flow (FCF): Cash generated by a company after accounting for operating expenses and capital expenditures. Essential for debt servicing in LBOs.

Financial Sponsor: A private equity firm or investment group that initiates and funds an LBO transaction.

G

Gross Margin: The percentage of revenue remaining after deducting the cost of goods sold (COGS).

Growth Equity: A type of private equity investment focused on minority stakes in high-growth companies.

H

High-Yield Bonds: Unsecured, high-interest debt instruments used in LBOs for additional leverage.

Hurdle Rate: The minimum rate of return required by investors to justify an investment.

I

Internal Rate of Return (IRR): The annualized rate of return earned by an investment, calculated using projected cash flows and the initial equity investment.

Interest Coverage Ratio: A metric indicating a company's ability to pay interest on its debt, calculated as EBITDA divided by interest expense.

J

Junk Bonds: High-yield bonds with lower credit ratings, often used in LBO financing.

K

Key Performance Indicators (KPIs): Metrics used to evaluate the performance and health of a business.

L

Leverage: The use of borrowed capital to amplify returns on equity. High leverage increases risk and reward.

Leveraged Buyout (LBO): An acquisition strategy where a significant portion of the purchase price is financed with debt.

M

Management Buyout (MBO): A type of LBO where the target company's management team acquires the business with financial backing.

Mezzanine Debt: A subordinated debt layer in the capital structure, offering higher interest rates and flexible terms.

Multiple Expansion: An increase in the valuation multiple (e.g., EV/EBITDA) during the ownership period, contributing to equity returns.

N

Net Present Value (NPV): The difference between the present value of cash inflows and outflows over a period of time.

Non-Recourse Debt: Debt secured by collateral, where lenders cannot pursue the borrower's other assets in case of default.

O

Operating Leverage: The degree to which a company's operating income is affected by changes in revenue. High fixed costs indicate higher operating leverage.

Option to Buy: A contractual right to purchase an asset at a predetermined price.

P

Private Equity (PE): A form of investment that involves buying and managing companies to increase their value and achieve high returns.

Purchase Price Multiple: A valuation metric that expresses the purchase price as a multiple of EBITDA or another financial measure.

Q

Quality of Earnings: An assessment of the sustainability and reliability of a company's earnings.

R

Return on Equity (ROE): A measure of financial performance, calculated as net income divided by shareholder equity.

Roll-Up Strategy: An acquisition strategy aimed at consolidating a fragmented industry by acquiring smaller companies.

S

Scenario Analysis: A technique to evaluate how different assumptions impact financial outcomes, such as IRR or valuation.

Senior Debt: Debt secured by the assets of a company, typically offering the lowest cost of capital.

Sensitivity Analysis: A method to determine how different variables impact a financial model's outputs.

Sponsor: The entity, often a private equity firm, initiating and executing an LBO.

T

Terminal Value: The estimated value of a business at the end of a projection period, often calculated using perpetuity growth or exit multiples.

Total Value Creation: The cumulative increase in a company's value during the ownership period, achieved through operational improvements, strategic growth, and multiple expansion.

U

Unitranche Debt: A single-layer debt structure combining senior and subordinated debt with a blended interest rate.

Unsecured Debt: Debt not backed by specific collateral, carrying higher risk and interest rates.

V

Value Creation Plan: A detailed strategy outlining how the sponsor will increase the target company's value post-acquisition.

Vendor Financing: A financing arrangement where the seller provides a loan to the buyer to facilitate the acquisition.

W

Weighted Average Cost of Capital (WACC): The average rate of return required by all investors in a company's capital structure, weighted by the proportion of each component.

Working Capital: Current assets minus current liabilities, representing the liquidity available to meet short-term obligations.

X

Exit Multiple: The valuation multiple (e.g., EV/EBITDA) applied at exit, influencing the realized equity returns.

Y

Yield to Maturity (YTM): The total return expected on a bond if held to maturity.

Z

Zero-Coupon Bond: A bond sold at a discount that pays no interest but redeems at face value at maturity.

Afterword

Embracing the Pinnacle of LBO Excellence

As we conclude the *Advanced LBO Masterclass*, this journey has been more than a deep dive into financial frameworks and deal mechanics. It is a strategic roadmap to mastering the multifaceted, high-stakes world of leveraged buyouts. From deal sourcing and valuation to ESG integration, AI-driven strategies, and innovative exit solutions, this masterclass equips you with the tools and insights to navigate and thrive in private equity's dynamic landscape.

At its core, private equity is about more than numbers. It's about creating lasting value, driving transformation, and impacting industries and communities. Success in leveraged buyouts demands a blend of strategic foresight, collaborative execution, and adaptability in the face of market complexities. As a graduate of this program, you join an elite cadre of professionals poised to lead and innovate in this ever-evolving sector.

The Path Forward

Your journey doesn't end here. In fact, it is just beginning. The private equity world will continue to evolve with advancements in technology, shifting market dynamics, and the growing emphasis on sustainability and ethical investing. Staying ahead requires a commitment to continuous learning, a bold approach to leadership, and a passion for pushing boundaries.

Let the knowledge and frameworks you've gained from this course serve as your foundation for navigating complexities, seizing opportunities, and making strategic decisions that leave an indelible impact. Whether you're an operating partner, a portfolio leader, or a rising star in private equity, the principles outlined in ALBOM will remain your compass for success.

Gratitude and Aspiration

This journey is a testament to your dedication to excellence. We express our gratitude to you—our participants—for embracing this program with enthusiasm and commitment. We also extend our thanks to the thought leaders, industry experts, and collaborators who contributed to the depth and relevance of this masterclass. Together, we aspire to continue fostering a culture of excellence, innovation, and value creation within the private equity ecosystem.

Final Reflections

Excellence in private equity is not a destination but a mindset. As you take your next steps, let the insights and tools from this masterclass guide your decisions, inspire your leadership, and drive your contributions to the field. Embrace challenges as opportunities, celebrate milestones, and remain steadfast in your pursuit of creating meaningful value.

Thank you for embarking on this transformative journey with us. The pinnacle of private equity excellence awaits you.

Here's to your continued success in shaping the future of leveraged buyouts and private equity.

Copyright Notice

VCII Institute
www.vciinstitute.com
Email: support@vciinstitute.org

Published by VCII

Explore More with VCII

At VCII, our mission is to empower professionals with world-class education and actionable insights. As a nonprofit organization, we are committed to democratizing access to knowledge, fostering growth, and supporting your journey toward professional excellence.

The *Advanced LBO Masterclass* is one of many transformative courses we offer. Explore a wide range of programs designed to enhance your expertise in leadership, value creation, digital transformation, and beyond. Whether you are an experienced professional or just beginning your journey, there is a course tailored to your ambitions.

We encourage you to visit our website and explore our full catalog of educational offerings. By enrolling in additional courses, you invest in your personal and professional growth while supporting our nonprofit mission to make quality education accessible to all.

Thank you for choosing VCII. Your dedication inspires us to continue developing impactful content that empowers individuals and transforms industries. Together, we can shape a brighter future.

Visit us today at www.vciinstitute.com.

www.ingramcontent.com/pod-product-compliance
Lightning Source LLC
LaVergne TN
LVHW080036210926
848481LV00011B/3212